Sedona:
The Essential
Guidebook

Enjoy Sedona!
Dennis Andres
"Mr. Sedona"

Dennis Andres

Meta Adventures Publishing
Sedona, Arizona

To order books contact:
Dreams In Action Distribution
928-204-1560
info@dreamsinaction.us
orders@dreamsinaction.us
website: www.dreamsinaction.us

2nd printing
ISBN-10 0-9721202-3-8
ISBN-13 978-09721202-3-4

Library of Congress
Catalog Card Number 2006933950

Printed in Canada

Table of Contents

Introduction

A Tale of Two Sedonas

During years of living and guiding here, I've noticed that opinions
from tourists about their experiences while visiting Sedona tend to
fall into two distinct categories. Their reports were so dramatically
different that it sounded as if they had actually been to two different
places.

While everyone agreed on Sedona's beauty, many found it hard to
access from behind the wheel of an auto. Some encountered friendly
locals, but others felt as if people were just trying to sell them something. The weather was just right for some, but too chilly (or too hot)
for the rest. Some were uplifted by Sedona's energy, while others had
no time to notice: They were in a hurry to get to Grand Canyon, or
back to a conference in Phoenix.

What produces such differing accounts? Do red rocks move? Do
locals pick and choose which tourists to be nice to? Do weather and
energy conspire to delight or disappoint? No, of course not. The
happier group gave Sedona more time, seeing it as a destination
rather than a place to pass through. They were also better informed,

by asking questions or consulting this very book. The final element, however, was something they brought with them that mattered far more than any mere item of luggage.

Their attitude.

Grateful for nature, appreciative visitors always seem to be the ones who discover special places among the red rocks. Hopeful yet patient, such people notice that the occasional clouds yield better sunsets, and summer rains bring magical rainbows. Because they think the best of everyone they meet, friendly tourists become valued guests, welcomed by an entire community. Instead of rushing to find energy spots, these adventurers pause to stand still, take a deep breath and let the good vibrations come to them.

As someone who has traveled the world, I know that such an outlook is a compass pointing to the greatest adventures and a key unlocking doors where the most fascinating people and sights await. If you will open your mind to great wonders and your heart to rich emotions, Sedona will fill both abundantly. It will show you that there are still places on Earth that raise the spirit and replenish the soul.

Afterward you will return home to recount to friends what a delightful Sedona visit you enjoyed. You might not even realize that the true secret of success wasn't weather or traffic, shops or circumstances. It was you.

Now, which Sedona will you visit?

— Dennis Andres
Sedona, Arizona

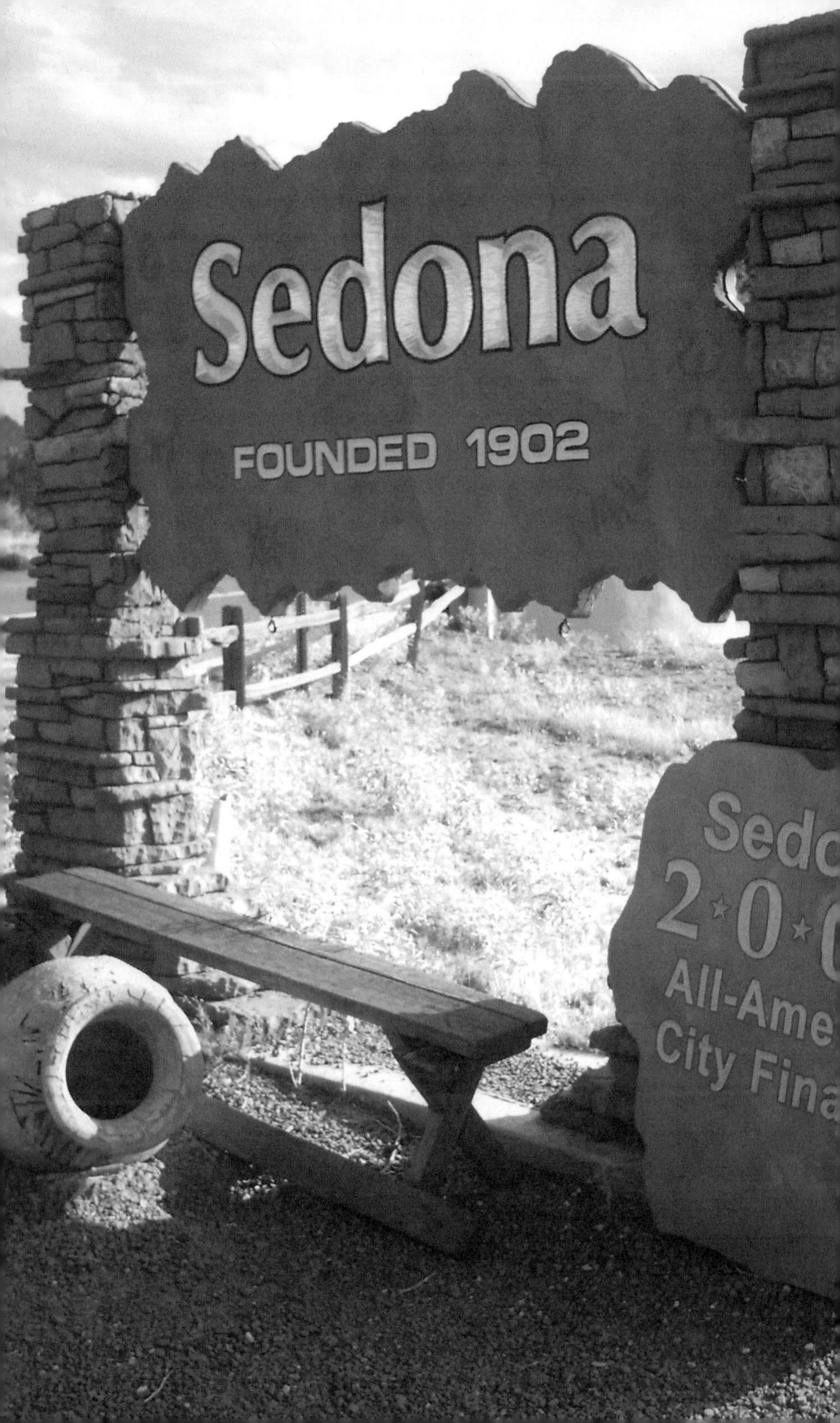
Sedona
FOUNDED 1902

1

The First Steps to the Perfect Trip

Weather

The general answer to the question "Which is the best time to visit Sedona?" is "Any time you can." That's not just a sales pitch: The weather here is truly pleasant for most of the year.

Spring and autumn are easy to describe: perfect. Deep blue sky and comfortable temperatures are typical. Along with the nice weather, there's lots to see in the outdoors. Spring wildflowers abound in a thrilling variety of colors. Balloonists should note that breezes can be strong on spring afternoons. Autumn means lovely foliage in Oak Creek Canyon. High elevation means low temperatures at night, so both spring and autumn nights are relatively cool.

What about winter? Cooler temperatures prevail, but generally it is still comfortable outside. Daytime highs in the mid 50s and up are standard, but with bright sunshine and no humidity, it feels much warmer here than elsewhere. (Although it gets windy, "wind chill" is an unknown term around here.) With a sweater or jacket, it's a wonderful time to be outdoors, and there are far fewer tourists. Note that winter brings curious weather days. Sedona typically receives three to five winter snowstorms, though the white stuff is usually melted from the streets by noon. High on the formations, however, it may remain beautifully visible for days. On the other hand, it isn't shocking to have days in the high 60s and above during the winter. If you're coming in March or April though, be aware of the annual "surprise" spring snowstorm, as well as unseasonably warm days. Regardless of what the day brings, winter nights are always cold, with temperatures dropping to freezing.

An Arizona saying states that we have six seasons: Autumn, Winter, Spring, Summer, Fire and Rain. The two-part summer begins early, with June temperatures typically in the 80s and 90s and with no precipitation or humidity whatsoever. In July and August comes the famous "monsoon," with late afternoon rainfalls that pelt the red rocks. Often the rains don't come at all, but when they do, they are welcome. Monsoon storms cool down temperatures, soak dry forests and bring amazing rainbows. If you're here in the summer, do what locals do. Get up early to take advantage of cool mornings. By the same token, note that the heat lingers late in the day. For outdoor activities, choose early morning over late afternoon.

AVERAGE TEMPERATURES

Elevation changes by more than a thousand feet between the entrance to Sedona at the Village of Oak Creek and the northern exit in the upper part of Oak Creek Canyon. That means canyon temperatures are five or more degrees cooler than in the heart of Sedona, which in turn can be a few degrees warmer than the Village.

Be aware that most web sites report Phoenix, Cottonwood or Flagstaff temperatures and label them "Sedona." Sedona is usually seven to ten degrees cooler than Phoenix, three to five degrees cooler than Cottonwood, and twelve to fifteen degrees warmer than Flagstaff. For the best results, check www.sedonaweather.net.

PRECIPITATION

High desert is a common phrase for the area's climate, though Sedona receives a bit too much precipitation to be considered a desert. Winter precipitation is as likely to come in the form of snowfall as rain. Sedona's annual precipitation average is 15.94 inches.

Average Temperatures (high/low) and Precipitation

January 1-14	55° / 29°	January 15-31	56° / 29°	2.10 inches
February 1-14	58° / 30°	February 15-28	60° / 31°	2.16 inches
March 1-14	62° / 33°	March 15-31	64° / 35°	2.47 inches
April 1-14	69° / 38°	April 15-30	73° / 40°	1.16 inches
May 1-14	78° / 44°	May 15-31	82° / 48°	0.71 inches
June 1-14	88° / 52°	June 15-30	93° / 56°	0.26 inches
July 1-14	96° / 61°	July 15-31	96° / 63°	0.89 inches
August 1-14	95° / 63°	August 15-31	93° / 62°	1.90 inches
September 1-14	90° / 59°	September 15-30	87° / 56°	1.94 inches
October 1-14	82° / 51°	October 15-31	77° / 46°	1.67 inches
November 1-14	69° / 40°	November 15-30	69° / 40°	0.38 inches
December 1-14	59° / 32°	December 15-31	55° / 29°	0.30 inches

Transportation

DIRECTIONS/DRIVE TIME TO SEDONA

From Phoenix Sky Harbor Airport: 2 hours, 5 minutes
Your options: simple, tricky and a change of view. For simple,
follow airport signs for I-17 north. You won't have to make another
turn for an hour and 45 minutes. Take exit 298 to Sedona/Oak
Creek. Turn left off the exit ramp and follow Hwy 179 for 7 miles
(8 minutes) to the Village of Oak Creek, and 15 miles (19 minutes)
to Uptown or West Sedona. Your return trip to the airport will be
faster, since it is all downhill. Faster still if there are two or more in

the car, in which case you
can take the HOV lane.
But plan for Phoenix rush
hours, which tend to begin
and end a bit earlier than
in the Midwest and East.

Now for tricky. From the
airport, follow signs for
I-10 east (crazy, I know).
Follow for 12 minutes,
moving to right-hand exit
lanes to get on I-17 north
(Flagstaff). As above, stay
on I-17 all the way to the
Sedona exit.

Make this trip often and
want a new route? Follow I-10 east just a few minutes to SR 51
north. Take 51 to 101 west, then I-17 north to the Sedona exit.

Been to Sedona and want to avoid the weekend crowds? Take I-17
North to Camp Verde and State Route 260 (exit 287), then west to
Cottonwood. Go North on Hwy 89A to Sedona. You'll arrive via the
west side of Sedona, rather than through the Village of Oak Creek.

From Scottsdale Resorts: 1 hour 50 minutes
Check with your concierge for best directions. Chances are, you'll
hop on SR 51 or Loop 101 heading north. If on 51, you'll choose
101 West. The 101 takes you to I-17, which you'll follow north for
90 minutes. Take exit 298 at Sedona/Oak Creek/179. Turn left off
the exit ramp and follow Hwy 179 for 7 miles (8 minutes) to the
Village of Oak Creek, and 15 miles (19 minutes) to Uptown or
West Sedona.

From Central Phoenix & Points South: 1 hour 55 minutes
Take I-17 North (Flagstaff) for 90 minutes. Take exit 298, turn left
off the exit ramp and follow Hwy 179 for 7 miles (8 minutes) to
the Village of Oak Creek, and 15 miles (19 minutes) to Uptown or
West Sedona.

From Flagstaff and Points North: 50 minutes
Dropping down the Colorado Plateau, you'll see scenic beauty and
lots of curves by following I-17 south (Phoenix/Sedona) for about
2 miles to the Sedona/Oak Creek Canyon/89A exit. (Careful at the
stop sign—oncoming traffic moves quickly on 89A.) If switchbacks
make you nervous, then stay on I-17 south for nearly 40 minutes,
and take the Sedona/Oak Creek/Hwy179 exit. Follow Hwy 179
north for 8 minutes to the Village of Oak Creek, and 19 minutes to
Uptown or West Sedona.

From Las Vegas, Nevada: 5 hours
Why do people come via Las Vegas? It's not the flight connections or
the gambling. That's where all the rental cars are. It's like some kind
of a giant rental car vortex. There's less to see than you would think
on this trip. Anyway, take I-93 over Hoover Dam (okay, that's one
thing to see) to I-40. Now's the time for a book on tape. After the
book has ended—four hours into your trip—take exit 195, I-17
south, to exit 337. Take a right off the ramp, then an immediate left
onto Hwy 89A. Twenty-eight winding miles later, you'll be here.
The bad news: no gambling here. The good news: no gambling here.

5

Getting to Sedona

By Plane to Phoenix

Though Phoenix's Sky Harbor International Airport is quickly becoming one of America's busier airports, it rarely has the snags of airports to the north. It is a little over a two-hour drive to Sedona. There are three terminals at this airport, numbered, confusingly, Terminals 2, 3 and 4.

SHUTTLE SERVICE

These services pick you up at or return you to any terminal at Phoenix's Sky Harbor Airport.

★ **The Extra Mile Express Shuttle** The friendly husband-and-wife duo that began this service keeps expanding, but the service is still based on reservations, rather than regular runs. They offer door-to-door service, traveling in vans and mini-vans. $55 per person one way, $98 round trip, cash or check only. Mon-Fri, 8:30am-5pm. Sat-Sun, 9am-12 noon. 928-649-9506, 866-356-3987. www.extramileexpress.com

Sedona Phoenix Shuttle has the largest fleet and the most regular runs, although reservations are nonetheless required. What would be a two-hour drive by car is always more than two hours in this shuttle because of stops in Camp Verde and Cottonwood, $45 per person one way, $85 round trip. Pickups at Phoenix Sky Harbor are at 10am, 11am, 12pm, 1pm, 2pm, 4pm, 6pm and 8pm, arriving more than two hours later in Sedona, and a little longer than that in the Village of Oak Creek. Check in at the InterCity Transportation Counter near the baggage claim at each terminal. From Sedona to the airport, departures are at 6am, 7am, 8am, 9am, 10am, 12 noon, 2pm and 4pm, arriving more than two hours later. (Village of Oak Creek departures are 20 minutes earlier in each case.) Closed on Thanksgiving and Christmas. Cash or traveler's check only. Call 928-282-2066, 1-800-448-7988 (toll-free only within Arizona).

Village of Oak Creek/La Quinta Hotel; West Sedona/Super 8 Motel, 928-282-1533, 2545 W. Hwy 89A. www.sedona-phoenix-shuttle.com
Ace-Xpress This company offers door-to-door service, and the travel time is sometimes shorter than the shuttle. They schedule pickup times around the initial booking. If you call early, there is a pretty good chance you'll get picked up in Sedona or at the airport relatively close to your ideal time. Cost is $47 per person one way, $78 round trip, cash or check only. 928-649-2720.

7

LIMOUSINE SERVICE
Luxury Limousine Ride in a white Town Car to or from the airport, $200, 928-204-0620. www.gatewaytosedona.com.
Sedona Limousines Call for airport rates. 928-204-1383, 800-775-6739.
White Tie Limousine Rates, one way and round trip, depend on which of their vehicles you request, but the ride is usually around $225 for one or two people in the Lincoln Town car. Vans are available. 928-203-4500. whitetietransportation.com

BUS SERVICE
There is currently no bus service to Sedona. Greyhound does run between Phoenix and Flagstaff, with a stop in Camp Verde, about 35 minutes south of Sedona.

Key to Symbols

★ = **Highly Recommended**
(($)) = **Great Value**

Renting a Car

CAR RENTALS IN PHOENIX

Thanks to the new Rental Car Center at Phoenix's Sky Harbor Airport, you'll no longer find your chosen car company in the terminal. Airport-based companies, including Advantage, Avis, Budget, Dollar, Enterprise, Hertz, National, Alamo, and Thrifty, all now use a common "rental car shuttle" bus. Other car rentals are located away from the airport, so check with them for pickup information upon arrival and get directions for the return.

To get to the Rental Car Center, take I-10 south off I-17 in Phoenix. Take the Washington/Jefferson St. exit 148. Go south (straight) on the frontage road to Sky Harbor Circle and turn right. Follow the signs to the facility. If instead you take I-17 all the way to the airport, your final mile will put you on I-10 heading northbound. Take exit 149 and turn left on Buckeye Road. Take Buckeye Road to to Sky Harbor Circle south and turn left. Follow signs to the facility. The bus trip to the terminal is five to eight minutes.

You can save some money and skip the "stadium tax" applied to car rentals in Phoenix by getting in a shuttle and renting locally.

CAR RENTALS

BTW Sedona Rent a Car Formerly "Practical Rent a Car of Sedona," they offer free local pickup and drop off, after hours service, group discounts, seasonal discounts and repair and insurance replacement with direct billing. You can leave the vehicle at Phoenix Sky Harbor Airport at the end of your trip, but the charge is $150. 2900 W Hwy 89A, Suite 6, WS. 928-282-0554, 877-467-8578.
Enterprise The national franchise is on the west side of town. 2090 W Hwy 89A, WS. 928-282-2052, 1-800-736-8222; out of town 1-800-325-8007.
Sedona Car Rental Compact, mid-size, full-size, SUV, jeeps and specialty vehicles are available for rent. CD audio tours and jeeps are available for self-guided tours. Free local pickup and customer drop-off are available. Open daily, 8am-5pm. Sedona Airport, 235 Air Terminal Drive, WS. 928-282-227, 800-879-5337.

JEEP RENTALS

Farabee's Jeep Rentals These folks rent Jeep Wranglers modified for off-roading, and they'll show you where to go too. Up to four hours is $125. Up to 12 hours is $185. Rentals include ice chest with ice, complete trail information, and instruction on using a Jeep. Tire/glass coverage costs $20 and insures you for the full value of one tire and all glass with no deductible. 3009 W Hwy 89A, WS. 928-282-8700.

9

A Day In The West The local tour company offers several different Jeeps for rent. Jeep Wrangler, $50/hr; Jeep Rubicon, $65/hr; modified Jeep Wrangler, $75/hr. All three have two-hour minimums. You can get the fourth hour free if you rent the standard Wrangler or the Rubicon for three hours. The modified Wrangler is $300 for four hours. Packages include a guide manual, maps of the area and a box lunch or sit-down meal at Orchards restaurant in Uptown. 252 N Hwy 89A, UP. 928-282-4320, 800-973-3662.

MOTORCYCLE RENTALS

Eagle Rider This Village of Oak Creek shop offers a selection of Harley-Davidson motorcycles. 6560 Highway 179 Suite 100, VOC. 928-284-3983, 866-392-0747.

Visitor Centers

Not all offices offering "tourist information" are what they appear. The Chamber of Commerce's official visitor centers are in Uptown at the corner of Forest Road and Hwy 89A, and in the Village of Oak Creek at Tequa Plaza. Plans are in place to level the current Uptown center and replace it with a new one. Hours are Mon-Sat, 8:30am-5pm, Sun and holidays 9am-3pm. Closed Christmas, Thanksgiving and New Year's Day. 928-282-7722, 800-288-7336. www.sedonachamber.com or www.visitsedona.com

Town Orientation

Is Sedona a small town or a big one? By population, it is small indeed, with around 15,000 residents. However, if you include the national forest and state parks of the area, Sedona stretches from north to south nearly 25 miles. So what's the best way to get a handle on it? Think of Sedona proper as having five parts and two major highways.

The Highways You need know only two figures: "179" and "89A." State Route 179 (better known as Hwy 179) runs from south to north, beginning at the exit from I-17 and running 15 miles through the Village of Oak Creek to Uptown Sedona. Hwy 179 ends as it reaches Highway 89A. This road extends west through the west side of Sedona, north through Uptown and into Oak Creek Canyon.

What do you really need to know about these parts of town when planning your visit? First, you can hardly make a poor choice. There are no "ugly" parts of Sedona! Likewise, all five areas offer choices for shopping, dining, accommodations and great outdoor adventures. These areas are Uptown, West Sedona, Below the "Y," Oak Creek Canyon, and Village of Oak Creek.

UP **UPTOWN** is the heart of Sedona, full of tours and T-shirts, but with an unexpectedly quiet neighborhood off the main strip. Running through Uptown is Hwy 89A, and along this lane pass most of the many passers-through on their way to the Grand Canyon. It is a departure point for many tours, and the home of many shops and galleries. In a sense, Uptown has the best and worst of all worlds: the most activity…and the most activity.

WS **WEST SEDONA** is the most residential part of town, home to major grocery stores, many of the town's finest restaurants and numerous hiking trails. While all five areas include public land for outdoor use, this area (to the town's legal borders and beyond) is especially large in forest terrain. Keep that in mind when traveling around. From Uptown to this area's nearest point (the post office) takes one minute in a car. To its most distant points can take 30 minutes, and you may be on a dirt road to get there.

BTY **BELOW THE "Y"** The intersection of Hwys 89A and 179 is known as the "Y" and is approximately seven miles from the Village of Oak Creek. This seven-mile stretch hosts more shopping, accommodations and trails but has never had a name acknowledged by the community as a whole. So everything from the "Y" south, we'll call **Below the "Y,"** representing territory on either side of Hwy 179 between the Village of Oak Creek and Uptown.

11

OCC **OAK CREEK CANYON,** a historic and beautiful area, flanks Hwy 89A as it winds north from Midgley Bridge to the switchbacks leading up the side of the Colorado Plateau. Full of ponderosa pines and tall cliffs, Oak Creek Canyon is more elevated in altitude than other parts of town. That makes it a splendid getaway in warm seasons, the center for foliage in autumn, and chilly enough for an occasional white Christmas once in a while in the winter.

VOC **VILLAGE OF OAK CREEK** is the unincorporated section that lies south of all these areas. If arriving from Phoenix, it is the first area you'll see. "The Village," as locals call it, now offers much more than the outlet mall, with expanding neighborhoods, two major golf courses and plenty of accommodations. It still features a few folks who spell it differently (Village of Oakcreek) or call it by another name, "Big Park." Separated from the other districts by a scenic seven-mile drive, this area offers the pros and cons of isolation. It means fewer crowds and more opportunities for quiet. However, it also means that you may find yourself "commuting" to town for more trail, tour and dining choices. So how bad is the commute? That depends on your attitude and your timing. The 10 to 15 minute trip is thoroughly pleasant if you're in the mood for fantastic scenery. On a busy Saturday, however, it may be less enjoyable when it takes 25 minutes, and you have to do it more than once.

To make things simple, we've labeled all addresses in this book to let you know immediately which part of Sedona they're in. You'll see these abbreviations throughout the book: **UP** (Uptown), **WS** (West Sedona), **BTY** (Below the "Y"), **OCC** (Oak Creek Canyon), and **VOC** (Village of Oak Creek).

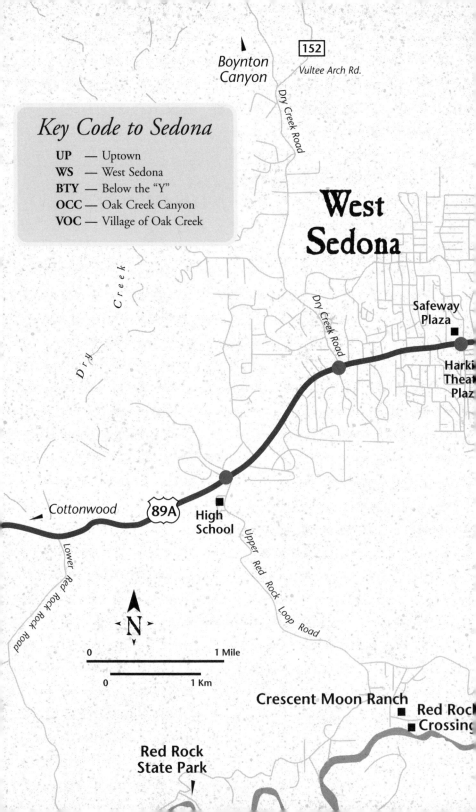

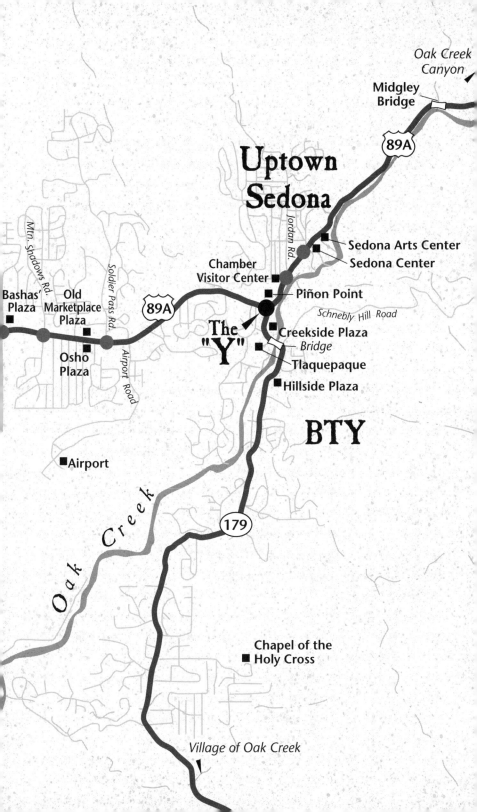

Harding Point +

Flagstaff

Cookstove Draw

Pine Flat
campground

West Fork

Cave Springs
campground

Oak Creek
Canyon

Call of the
Canyon

89A

East Pocket
Knob +

Surveyor Canyon

Bootlegger
campground

Banjo Bill
campground

Oak Creek

Slide Rock
State Park

Manzanita
campground

Lost Wilson
Mountain +

Encinoso
picnic area

Trout Farm

Wilson Mountain

Dairy
Queen

Munds
Canyon

Indian
Gardens

N

0   1 Mile

0   1 Km

Wilson Canyon

89A

Shiprock +

Casner Canyon

Steamboat +

Midgley
Bridge

Grasshopper
Point

Sedona

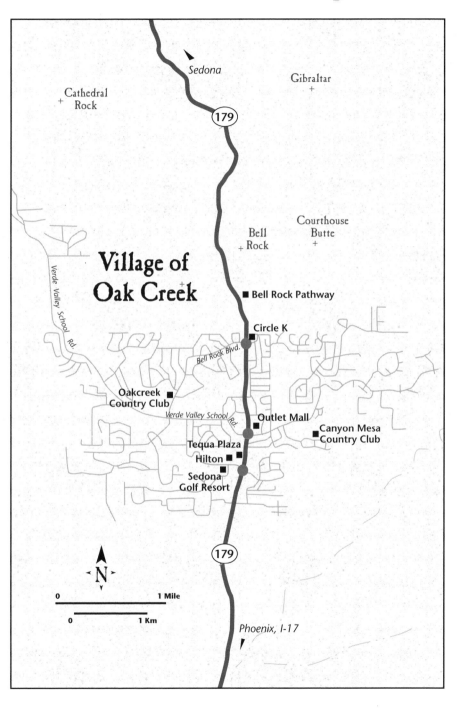

Sedona

Gibraltar
+

Cathedral
+ Rock

179

Courthouse
Butte
+

Bell
+ Rock

Village of Oak Creek +

■ Bell Rock Pathway

Verde Valley School Rd.

■ Circle K

Bell Rock Blvd.

Oakcreek ■
Country Club

Verde Valley School Rd.

■ Outlet Mall

Canyon Mesa
■ Country Club

Tequa Plaza ■
Hilton ■

Sedona
Golf Resort

N

| 0 | 1 Mile |
| 0 | 1 Km |

179

Phoenix, I-17

Annual Events

FEBRUARY

The Sedona Marathon Here's your chance to run through "America's Most Beautiful Place." The route is on the west side of town into the Coconino National Forest on dirt roads in very scenic country. Includes a 5K fun run and a half-marathon. The inaugural marathon in 2006 hosted approximately 150 marathoners, and a thousand overall runners. Expect it to grow. Held on the second Saturday in February. 800-775-7561. www.SedonaMarathon.com

★ The Sedona International Film Festival This is a marvelous chance for locals and visitors to sample the best of the world's independent productions. The "Sundance of Arizona" has done remarkably well with independent American and foreign movies that won't be showing at the movieplex in your mall. Founded in 1994, the festival screens more than 100 films. Individual flicks can be viewed for $10 at Harkins Theatres, but day and weekend passes are available. If money is no object, attend the gala event on Friday night, usually held at Enchantment Resort. Someone from Hollywood is sure to be there. Last weekend in February. 928-282-1177. www.sedonafilmfestival.com

MARCH

St. Patrick's Day Parade Held in the Uptown area, typically on the Saturday closest to March 17. There's a 5K run before the parade starts. It's a fun day when the town in the Red Rocks dresses up green. Jordan Road, UP. 928-282-0747.

APRIL

Verde Valley Birding and Nature Festival Dead Horse Ranch State Park in Cottonwood is the primary venue, but Sedona's Red Rock State Park and Slide Rock State Park also participate in this nature show. The festival is held on April's final weekend and includes field trips, workshops and of course, bird counts. Over 171 species were seen in three days last year. Field trips during the festival weekend have included visiting the Grand Canyon to see condors, viewing birds from the Verde Canyon Railroad train, and "power birding" in Prescott. For information, call Barbie Hart at 928-282-2002 or the special line at Parks and Recreation for the City of Cottonwood, 928-634-8437. www.birdyverde.org

★ **The Sedona Art & Sculpture Walk** This annual event features the work of more than 100 sculptors in a special juried event. Although timing and location have changed, the Sculpture Walk has been chugging along for over 17 years. Traditional and innovative materials and styles are showcased, including sculptural works in clay, glass, bronze, wood, marble, neon and found objects. Other fine art mediums include oil, watercolor, acrylics, photography and glass mosaic. The art ranges from small to tall. The 2006 event was held at the end of April at the Radisson Poco Diablo on Hwy 179. This event is organized by the Sedona Arts Center. 928-282-3809, 888-954-4442. www.sedonasculpturewalk.com

17

MAY

The Sedona Century Bicycle Tour This charity bicycle challenge winds though beautiful Sedona and the surrounding Verde Valley. The ride features two routes: a Metric Century and a 40-mile distance. Registration fee includes an official T-shirt, full ride support, rest stops, lunch and massage. Festivities also include contests and prizes, and a Friday night mixer hosted by Absolute Bikes of Sedona. Usually held on the first Saturday in May. 928-284-1242, 877-284-1272.

★ **Chamber Music Sedona** For years, this organization has offered a series of concerts with an exceptional record of hosting both U.S. and international performers. Most events are held in spring and autumn. 928-204-2415. www.chambermusicsedona.org

Northern Arizona Watercolor Show This show, sometimes held at Tlaquepaque, is a presentation of the Northern Arizona Watercolor Society. This twice yearly event features the work of up to 20 members. You can meet the artists and purchase original works. May and October, each year. Check with the Sedona Arts Center for information on the society, 928-282-3809, 888-954-4442. www.sedonaartscenter.org

ZGI Independent Filmmaking Gala Students at Sedona's Zaki Gordon Institute for Independent Filmmaking show off their final projects. This gives you the chance to see the work of students-turned-filmmakers in the intensive two-year program. Most movies are shorts, and the best ones are very entertaining. It is usually held on the third weekend in May. 928-649-4265. www.zaki.yc.edu

Sedona Garden Tour The Sedona Area Garden club sponsors this event, usually held around Mother's Day. 928-204-9050, 928-284-5574.

JUNE

Sedona Art & Architecture Tour See great views, great art and great homes that offer them in this popular tour. 928-204-6401, 928-282-4740.

Sedona Taste While it may not be summer on the calendar, it certainly is hot enough by the second weekend of June to think of it that way. That's when the Sedona Taste takes place, a fundraiser for the Boys and Girls Club featuring fantastic food and wine tasting. The shaded grounds give some relief from the heat. Two things are always found at this event: a great time and lots of overeating. Los Abrigados Resort. 928-282-7822. www.losabrigados.com

JULY

★ **Shakespeare Sedona** The performances are concurrent with an institute dedicated to teaching the Bard to aspiring writers and actors. Performances are often held outdoors during cooler evening hours at Tlaquepaque or indoors at Red Rock High School. 928-282-0747, 800-768-9286 www.shakespearesedona.com

Sedona Open Golf Championship The tournament is now four years old and has both professional and amateur divisions. It is held during the third weekend in July at the Oak Creek Country Club. 690 Bell Rock Boulevard. 928-284-1660. www.sedonaopen.com

Sedona Miniature Golf Championship No kidding, people actually fly here to play for genuine prize money or just good fun. Call the spa or concierge desk at Los Abrigados, the championship host. 928-282-1777. www.losabrigados.com

SEPTEMBER

Moonlight Madness Street Festival and Sidewalk Held on Saturday of Labor Day Weekend from noon to 9pm, this street festival includes free music and entertainment, children's activities, and sidewalk sales in numerous locations along Hwy 89A in Uptown Sedona. Sidewalk sales and some of the entertainment continue throughout the Labor Day weekend.

Airport Day and Car Show Airplanes, activities and community booths highlight this event on Airport Mesa. The Sedona Airport turned 50 years old in 2005. There are discount airplane rides, food and beverages, displays, and some airplane flybys as well as over 100 classic autos competing for prizes. Contact Al Comello at 928-862-0210 or al@comello.net

Fiesta del Tlaquepaque This celebration of Mexico's independence from Spain includes food, music, dance, and entertainment on the grounds of a shopping galleria designed to look like a Mexican city. Past acts have included Mexican rodeo-style roping, flamenco dancers and musicians, a traditional dance ensemble in colorful handmade costumes, and folk music from Latin America with a repertoire of rhythms on indigenous instruments. And mariachis, of course! There are lots of artist demonstrations, as well as food and a beer garden. Shuttle service is provided by Sedona Trolley every 15 minutes from 10am to 6pm, with pickup and drop-off in the Uptown Municipal Parking Lot at the corner of Schnebly and Sunset. Admission is free. Held on the closest weekend to mid-September. 928-282-4838. www.tlaq.com

★ **Jazz On The Rocks** One of Sedona's most successful annual events, Jazz On The Rocks is more than a quarter-century old. It begins Thursday evening with a private show, followed by a Friday night concert, a full day of jazz on Saturday, and the jazz brunch on Sunday. Past celebrities have included Chuck Mangione, Earl Klugh and Spyro Gyra. Proceeds benefit music education programs. Held on the final weekend in September. Tickets go on sale June 1, approximately $50 for Friday evening, $70 for lawn seating all day on Saturday. 1487 W. Hwy 89A, Suite 9. 928-282-1985. www.sedonajazz.com

OCTOBER

★ **The Sedona Arts Festival** This major festival, held on the second weekend in October, features excellent artists from around the country, but the Southwestern focus is naturally the best. Expect every hotel room in town to be booked if you don't call in advance. Sat-Sun, 10am-5pm. $5. Red Rock High School athletic field, corner of Hwy 89A and Upper Red Rock Loop Road, WS. 928-204-9456. www.sedonaartsfestival.com

Halloween The end of October is the chance for all Sedona's weirdos (I count myself among them) to let out their alter ego in our favorite holiday of the year, Halloween. I often wonder if the kids here develop an inferiority complex from seeing how amazingly decked out the adults get! Head to Uptown in costume for the fun. Sedona Main Street Program. www.sedonamainstreet.com

DECEMBER

20 **Bed and Breakfast Tour** Sponsored by the Premier Bed and Breakfasts of Sedona Association, this event raises funds donated to the Verde Valley Caregivers Coalition. The tour includes 14 B&Bs offering yummy refreshments. All ticket holders are entered in raffles that include overnight stays and numerous prizes. In addition, ticket holders receive discounts at local restaurants. Contact Almira Wagley, 800-788-2082, 928-284-0082. www.bbsedona.com

★ **The Festival of Lights** This fine tradition involves the lighting of 6,000 luminarias in Tlaquepaque's courtyards and walkways. Performances by carolers, musicians, and dancers take place from afternoon until dark, with the whole community participating in the lighting. Held 12 to 14 days before Christmas Day. Admission is free. 336 Hwy 179, BTY. 928-282-4838. www.tlaq.com

The Red Rock Fantasy of Lights If you're like me, you'd rather watch other people put up Christmas lights than do it yourself. Add a little hot chocolate and bring kids and this can actually be fun. The light show begins the weekend before Thanksgiving and finishes after New Year's. Forty five displays and more than one million lights are featured at this annual holiday show. Los Abrigados Resort, 160 Portal Lane, BTY. 928-282-1777. www.losabrigados.com

MONTHLY EVENTS

1st Friday Evening in the Galleries This monthly event features the finest galleries and artwork in Sedona. Participating galleries stay open late and host special events and openings the first Friday of every month. Stop by the Visitor Center in Uptown for a map of galleries, or start anywhere in Hillside or Tlaquepaque shopping gallerias. Sponsored by the Sedona Gallery Association.

ADDITIONAL EVENTS INFORMATION

The Sedona-Oak Creek Chamber of Commerce has an event calendar on its website. 928-282-7722. www.sedonachamber.com

Sedona Arts Center is worth a visit for its member gallery alone. It also features a gallery shop and hosts events and exhibits throughout the year including the Sedona Sculpture Walk. North end of Uptown at 15 Art Barn Road. 928-282-3809, 888-954-4442.

Sedona Creative Life Center hosts speakers, seminar leaders, movies, concerts and other events. 928-282-9300. www.sedonacreativelife.com

The Red Rock Review has an extensive calendar of events and can be found free of charge all around town. www.redrockreview.com

Sedona Monthly is a magazine with an events calendar. www.sedonammonthly.com

The Scene and *Kudos* are weekly events guides published by local newspapers and can often be found at hotels around town.

Four Corners is a bimonthly magazine with a calendar of spiritual/ New Age events for the Southwest, including Sedona.

Sedona Magazine is a glossy quarterly with an events calendar and gallery guide.

21

What Time Is It, Anyway?

Arizonans do not change their clocks, so you'll always find Sedona on Mountain Standard Time—except for the Navajo Reservation. This means that when the rest of the country is on Daylight Savings Time (April through October), Arizona time is three hours behind the East Coast and even with the Pacific Coast. When the country is on Standard Time (November through March), Arizona is one hour ahead of California, and two hours behind New York.

All times listed in this book are
Mountain Standard Time.

History

When it comes to the history of Sedona, you can go back or you can go way, way back. For a more in-depth history, including that of native peoples, check the essays in the final section of the book. For now, here's a brief summary of modern Sedona.

22 IT'S ALL IN THE NAME

Most Sedonans trace the history of the town to the date it got its name, 1902, although legendary Bear Howard and others had already settled in Oak Creek Canyon by this time. A Missourian settler named Ellsworth Schnebly invited his brother T.C. Schnebly to join him. Not long after, "T. Carl" and his wife arrived and established a farm near what is today the heart of town. Carl wrote to the U.S. Postal Service to petition for a town post office, suggesting "Oak Creek Crossing" or "Schnebly Station" as names.

Thank goodness, the U.S.P.S. turned him down. "Something shorter, that fits on a cancellation stamp," was the reply from Washington. At this point Ellsworth recommended T. Carl's wife as the town's namesake, in praise of her fine moral character. In 1902 Sedona Arabella Miller Schnebly lent this place her name.

Sedona pioneer "Bear" Howard settled near West Fork

HOLLYWOOD ARRIVES

Although the Schneblys' home would become the first of many B&Bs to come, it was writer and adventurer Zane Grey who would put the area on the map. Grey realized that books were good, but books-turned-into-screenplays could be far more lucrative. With the filming of his *The Call of The Canyon* in Oak Creek Canyon, the romance of Hollywood and the red rocks had begun. That era continued through the 1940s, 1950s and 1960s, with many stars passing through, including Jimmy Stewart,

The Call of the Canyon

By ZANE GREY

Harper & Brothers · Established 1817

Zane Grey brought the movies to Sedona with the filming of Call of the Canyon.

Judy Garland, Robert Mitchum, Henry Fonda and John Wayne. Heck, even Elvis made a movie here. (*Stay Away Joe* was its name, and apparently, everyone did.)

Although most celebrity artists came and went, other lesser-known actors and artists stayed, giving Sedona the moniker "artist colony." Just as critical as the exposure that movies brought was what was going on underneath the surface. In contrast to everyone's expectations, they found water. Sedona could not only be filmed, it could be settled.

23

NEW AGE SEDONA

With the personal growth movements of the 1970s and 1980s, the New Age found its Mecca in Sedona. Although people had been coming for years to connect to the energy of this place, the energy now had a brand name: vortex. You can bet a lot of arguments ensued (and continue today), but the contribution of New Agers made a difference. In a sense, their greatest contribution was to elevate Sedona's mystique to a level of spiritual significance. "It's not just a pretty place," they said. "It's a powerful one."

The population was finally in the thousands (rather than the hundreds) and growing inexorably. By now the formula for success was being worked out. Spectacular beauty and an ethereal feeling continued to draw in cowboys, artists and psychics, but more than anyone else, tourists!

SEDONA TODAY

Members of these groups and descendants of these eras are still here today: great-grandchildren of settler families and old cowboy stunt doubles; landscape painters and graphic designers; alternative healers and intuitive counselors; and Hollywood stars of the past. Add to this, timeshare salespeople and architects, passers-through driving

Jeep tours until something more stable comes along, and the ultra-wealthy buying a third home to visit for a few weeks each year. They live in a happy, tolerant town, and their values seem to be mixing. The Cowboy Artists of America got their start here, and many of those Reiki healers are selling timeshares to pay the bills. Meanwhile, visitors keep coming.

24

How to Speak Sedonan

Want to blend in more with the locals? Here's a primer on the local dialect.

First, use the word **energy** as often as possible. As in, "Wow, your energy is great today," and "Hmm, the energy seems to have changed since my last visit." In fact, whenever you're uncertain how to review food, music, living quarters or nature spots, draw on the "e" word.

Note local vocabulary. The word **money** is far too droll. We prefer "abundance" or "prosperity." When a New Age event requests a "love energy donation," don't worry, it's not sexual.

Know which topics to discuss. Popular chit-chats cover how lucky we are to live here, the joy of precipitation in any form, and the loveliness of last night's sunset. Sound hip by examining whether Sedona is "the next Aspen," and intellectual by analyzing whether or not that's a good thing. Meanwhile, stay away from "the alternate route," and other topics on the trade-off of a pretty nature spot for a new road. A fist fight could ensue.

Finally, know your pronunciations. The shopping galleria, **Tlaquepaque**, sounds like *tlah-keh-pah-keh*, although *tlah-keh-pah-kee* is acceptable. **Palatki** is the ancient ruin, not a New York governor, and is pronounced *pa-LAHT-kee*. Soften the "g" when naming the ancient peoples of the area, the **Sinagua** (sin-a-wa), but harden your consonants for the Mediterranean restaurant **Cuccina Rustica** (koo-chee-na ROO-stee-ka).

Good luck, and by the way, your energy looks great!

The next ten years will decide a lot. Will we be "Aspenized," i.e., divided further into underpaid transients on the one hand and wealthy snowbirds on the other? Will there be enough water? How wide should the roads be, and more broadly, how many visitors and future residents should they bring in? Will our individual desires for a home on the hillside overwhelm the community interest of protecting the views? And most of all, will the prize of being named America's Most Beautiful Destination (*USA Today*, 2003) be our greatest blessing or our worst nightmare?

The outcome of your visit to Sedona is just as exciting a question. The impression visitors have of Sedona seems to depend a great deal on what it is they seek. Chicagoans find it the very essence of outdoor beauty, while residents of nearby Flagstaff scoff at our commercialization of it. Californians find our oasis of positive energy splendid, but old-time Phoenix residents lament a Sedona that once was. Many Arizonans have never even been here, and yet everyone on Manhattan's Upper West Side seems to be scheduling a trip. On the same Uptown strip where an old-timer will scoff at the crowd, a newcomer will look up and be moved by the beauty of the rocks. Which Sedona will you see?

One thing is certain. Sedona should be appreciated NOW, while we've got it. This is a magical place and worthy of appreciation.

MORE ON SEDONA HISTORY
★ **Sedona Heritage Museum** If Sedona's past is of interest to you, try this local attraction. The history of the area from 1870 through 1950 is a primary focus. 735 Jordan Road, UP. 928-282-7038.

Want to Hear a Story?

Michael Peach, a jeep guide and actor, brings the history of Sedona and the Verde Valley to life through humor, song, cowboy poetry, and impersonations. Call the **Sedona Heritage Museum** for details, 928-282-7038.

Lodge
&
Registration

2

Your Guide to Accommodations

The very best thing happening in Sedona tourism is not that people visit. It's that more and more of those who visit are staying. For years, the average visit here could be measured in hours rather than days, fueled by a desire not to see Sedona, but in hopes of a scenic route to the Grand Canyon. In that equation, both sides lost. The town gained traffic, not true guests, and visitors didn't really see Sedona: They missed it.

28

The second-best thing happening is that for people who stay, the choices are better than ever. There are more rooms-with-views, more amenities and finer cuisine associated with accommodations today than at any time since Sedona Schnebly hosted visitors in her own home. As was probably true then too, service varies, but a lack of training in the hospitality industry is often overcome by friendliness.

A WORD ON OUR RATINGS

These days, it's no longer possible to tell what the guy in the airplane seat next to you paid for it. It's becoming like that with hotels. So to avoid listing a range such as "$195-$1,050," the price categories are based on an average of the room rates for two adults in the spring and autumn tourist seasons. In your calculations, consider the Sedona lodging tax, which has not been included.

You'll find higher and lower rates at nearly every spot, especially B&Bs and resorts. Deals are often available for summer and winter: Call the property or check out its website for details. Finally, although owners prefer to say they have cottages, villas, suites or "creekhouses," all are listed here simply as "rooms."

Recall our district labels (**WS**: West Sedona, **UP**: Uptown, **BTY**: Below the "Y," **OCC**: Oak Creek Canyon, **VOC**: Village of Oak Creek). For complete descriptions of each, check out "Town Orientation," page 10.

Meanwhile, if you'd like someone else to do the work, consider calling the folks at Sedona Central Reservations. They are paid by the hotel, so there's no cost to you. Their number is 800-445-4128.

$400 and above

Adobe Grand Villas Can a place be both opulent and intimate? Each suite's bathroom is big enough to have its own zip code, yet the pool seems like your own private pond. Splendid breakfasts are included, and private dining can be arranged. Views are limited. 14 rooms, $399-$725. 35 Hozoni Drive, WS. 928-203-7616. www.adobegrandvillas.com

29

Enchantment Resort If pleasure and scenery are the only criteria, Enchantment Resort is unmatched in Sedona. Magnificent Boynton Canyon is an exceptional setting: You're not looking at canyons in the distance...you're in one. The pools, tennis courts, croquet pitch, good dining and a lovely spa complete the setup. Activities include wine tastings and talks at the spa. Location is a few minutes out of town, which most guests like just fine. 220 rooms, $395-$940. 525 Boynton Canyon Road, WS. 928-282-2900, 800-826-4180. www.enchantmentresort.com

Mii Amo Spa at Enchantment Resort At Mii Amo, it's not a stay: it's a journey. The spa's "Journey Programs" refers to the three-, four- and seven-day stay plans offered, each of which includes accommodations, meals, treatments and other goodies. The spa's questionnaire helps them to help you plan the appropriate mix, as detailed (with meal times and classes planned) or as relaxed as you like. 16 rooms, three days (Thursday night arrival), $1,740-$2,940; four days (Sunday night arrival), $1,950-$3,450; seven days (arrival Thursday or Sunday night), $6,090. 800-826-4180. www.miiamo.com

Tip...Phone Numbers

Here's a quick tip on numbers. It is generally true that numbers with a 203, 204 or 282 prefix are for locations in Uptown and West Sedona. Numbers with a 284 prefix are in the Village of Oak Creek. There are exceptions, such as when someone moves a personal residence from one side of town to another.

$275-399

Briar Patch Inn Serene and natural are the tones at the Briar Patch, Sedona's most in-tune-with-its-surroundings inn. The cabins are rustic, and there are no phones in the rooms. If you can stand what you're missing, you'll love what you're getting in this peaceful setting along Oak Creek. During warmer months, enjoy live music during breakfast along the creek, or take a morning yoga class on the lawn. 18 rooms, $189-$389. 3190 N Hwy 89A, OCC. 928-282-2342, 888-809-3030. www.briarpatchinn.com

El Portal El Portal is more than a fine inn: It is a building of significance, with architecture and décor that deserve attention. You can admire both while dining on splendid cuisine prepared at breakfast, served daily, or at dinners on weekend nights. Tlaquepaque village is next door, and guide "Benny" Benedict is available for adventures farther beyond. Worst part about El Portal? Making a left turn onto Hwy 179. Best part? You probably won't want to leave. 12 rooms, $225-$495. Winter specials offer considerable discounts. Pet-friendly. 95 Portal Lane, BTY. 928-203-9405, 800-313-0017. www.innsedona.com

Highlight

More than two-thirds of Arizona's highest-rated bed & breakfast accommodations are located in Sedona, and the competition among them benefits you. You'll usually enjoy a multiple-course breakfast and an *hors d'ouevres* hour as well. Innkeepers can also be a good source of advice about the restaurant and tour choices you're making. Check the Sedona B&B Guild at www.bbsedona.net

L'Auberge de Sedona Sedona's urbane alternative offers French Country cottage-style accommodations, and complements them with outstanding food, which you can eat creekside when the weather is right. The restaurant's success has endured management changes. The less expensive Orchards complex is located on the lively Uptown strip, rather than by the secluded creek. Pet-friendly. 58 rooms, $259-$459. 301 L'Auberge Lane, UP. 800-272-6777. www.lauberge.com

30

$200-$274

This price range is clearly Sedona's sweet spot: No other has such a high number of quality accommodations. It is broken down by accommodation type.

INNS AND B&BS

Alma de Sedona Newer than most of Sedona's prestige inns, Alma has a spacious feel. You can breakfast by the pool, or watch the sunset there in the evening. Nearly all rooms include Jacuzzi tubs. 12 rooms, $149-$265. 50 Hozoni Drive, WS. 928-282-2737, 800-923-2282. www.almadesedona.com

Canyon Villa This B&B should simply give the rooms away for free, but charge for the view of Bell Rock. Honestly, you'll walk out to the pool and swim in a postcard. Smart guests take advantage of the outings of friendly and knowledgeable guide Mike Krajnak. 11 rooms, $189-$304. 40 Canyon Circle Drive, VOC. 928-284-1226. www.canyonvilla.com

Garland's Oak Creek Lodge When Garland's is open (April through mid-November), you'll dine in heaven and sleep in paradise here, with no TVs or telephone to disturb you in this ultimate canyon retreat. The lodge has the only clay tennis court for miles. Chef Amanda Stine pleases all comers. There's a very long waiting list and a two-night minimum, but it is worth a try. Your best hope is to check their website for cancellations, most of which occur during the week. Dinner is included in the $190-$225 rates, but not a 15 percent gratuity. 8067 N Hwy 89A, OCC. 928-282-3343. www.garlandslodge.com

Lodge at Sedona This inn's Mission Style has added touches that perfect the comfortable feel. Take a stroll in the labyrinth. Can you beat their full breakfasts on the patio on a sunny day? Not likely. Enjoy this central location without feeling stuck in the crowd. 14 rooms, $170-$325. Kallof Place, WS. 928-204-1942, 800-619-4467. www.lodgeatsedona.com

The Wishing Well Set on a hill just past Uptown, this small and private spot offers nice views. Enjoy breakfast wheeled into your room and private outdoor spas. 5 rooms, $205-225. N Hwy 89A, UP. 928-282-4194, 800-728-9474. www.sedonawishingwell.com

HOTELS & RESORTS

Amara Resort The class is back in Uptown. Amara Resort has somehow managed to be secluded and close to the action at the same time. Valet parking, a Mercedes for a shuttle, an art gallery for a lobby and a path to the creek add to the experience. Here, you can dine, swim, meditate or get married under happy Snoopy Rock. The resort has a non-chlorine pool, a fitness room, and excellent food at the restaurant, yet the beds get the best reviews. $179-$259. 310 N Hwy 89A, UP. 928-282-4828, 866.455.6610. www.amararesort.com

The Junipine Resort Nine miles up Oak Creek Canyon, this lodge has setting as its best feature. The resort rests along the creek, with towering ponderosa pines giving it a cooler, greener feel than resorts in town. The suite-size rooms are a good value, and are best taken advantage of by families with children or by multiple couples staying together. The restaurant deck is lovely in summer. It is also close to two of Sedona's most scenic spots, Slide Rock State Park and the West Fork trail. 50 rooms, $180-$255 for one room, two rooms $250-$320. 8351 N Hwy 89A, OCC. 928-282-3375, 800-742-7463. www.junipine.com

Sedona Rouge Hotel & Spa Beds to die for, exotic showers and mounted flat screen TVs are among the highlights of Sedona's newest major property. Somehow, the mélange of influences in the design— North African, Mediterranean, Spanish—fits in the red rocks. Amenities include a pool and fitness room, and the restaurant is Sedona's newest dining success. West-side location is central, but diminishes the views. 77 rooms, $189-$249. 2250 W Hwy 89A, WS. 928-203-4111. www.sedonarouge.com

CABINS

(($)) Crescent Moon Cabin is a three-bedroom, three-bathroom ranch house by Oak Creek that sleeps up to 10 people. There is a large living room with a wood-burning stove, also a sun porch and two kitchens. The cabin comes with the appliances you'll need, plus a barbecue grill and picnic table outside. Visit the web page of the Coconino National Forest for details. The cabin can be reserved up to six months in advance. No pets. $200 per night. National Recreation Reservation Service, 877-444-6777. www.reserveusa.com

$150-199

For more options in this range, try the lower-priced rooms at B&Bs listed above, or the suites of properties such as Sky Ranch Lodge, listed below.

Lantern Light Inn If what you most enjoy is making friends with locals, the friendliest locals around are the folks at this B&B. Hospitality here is always just right: They are happy to offer lots of advice, or leave you in peace and quiet. 4 rooms, $135-$295. 3085 W Hwy 89A, WS. 928-282-3419. www.lanternlightinn.com

33

$100-149

Canyon Wren Cabins A friend of mine spent her honeymoon at the deluxe suite at this Oak Creek Canyon getaway. The marriage didn't last, but the memories did. 4 cabins, $150-$165. 6425 N Hwy 89A, OCC. 928-282-6900. 800-437-9736. www.canyonwrencabins.com

Grace's Secret Garden B&B Located a few miles off the beaten path, Grace's little secret is out. 3 rooms, $125-$150. Pet friendly. 1240 Jacks Canyon Road, VOC. 928-284-2340, 800-597-2340. www.gracessecretgarden.com

Quail Ridge Resort is excellent for families, a couple of couples, or any situation where more than two people want to stay more than one night. The chalets have kitchens, and there is easy access to the national forest. Quail Ridge is on the same block as the fancy Graham and Canyon Villa B&Bs but far less expensive. It has a tennis court, pool and barbecue pit too. Housekeeping service is available by request, for a fee. Weekly rates available. $111-$194. 120 Canyon Circle Drive. 928-284-9327. www.quailridgeresort.com

Radisson Poco Diablo This mid-range resort offers a small executive golf course and pleasant views. Nearby is the Twin Buttes formation, backdrop for the Western *Broken Arrow,* starring Jimmy Stewart. $119-$199. 1752 S Hwy 179, BTY. 928-282-7333, 800-333-3333. www.radisson.com/sedonaaz.

$75-$99

(($)) **Sky Ranch Lodge** You heard it here: this is the best deal in town. Tremendous views a few feet away, pool, hot tub and quiet garden. God bless them for keeping their rates the same every day of the year. Pet-friendly. 94 rooms, $75-$189. Located at the top of Airport Road, WS. 928-282-6400; 888-708-6400. www.skyranchlodge.com

34

The Matterhorn Lodge Located on the Uptown strip, this motel offers a 20 percent discount for people over 62 on their first night's stay. They are pet-friendly too. A Triple-A 3-diamond property. $79-$159. 800-372-8207

Under $75

Sugar Loaf Lodge Reliably inexpensive and easy to find. Pet-friendly. $45-$72, 14 rooms. 1870 W Hwy 89A, WS. 928-282-9451, 877-282-0632. www.sedonasugarloaf.com

Red Rock Lodge This money-saving option is north of the Uptown strip. 8 rooms, $45-$99, $149 for a very large room that can sleep up to six people, 901 N Hwy 89A, UP. 928-282-3591. www.redrocklodge.com

Big Mistake

Ironically, while views are generous across Sedona, they're not guaranteed at your accommodation. So don't assume the pretty website photos are the same scenes you'll be seeing from your room. Call to find out which views (if any) the property really has, and which rooms have them. With few exceptions however, the best views in Sedona are seen from the outdoors, not the indoors.

Increasingly, pet-friendly isn't just possible, it's stylish. For a complete list, see the "Pets" section of the Personal Services chapter.

Prefer hotels of the leading national chains? Sedona's got them too. Best Western (we've got two of these), Days Inn, Hampton Inn, La Quinta, Super 8 and Quality Inn. For details, contact the national websites.

Vacation Rentals and Retreat Homes

There are lots of opportunities on the internet if you'd like to rent a private home. In most cases, this is a good way to get a good deal and a place of your own. Leasing agents can help too.

35

J.B. Jochum & Associates This long-time agency's website lists both short-term vacation rentals and long-term rentals. 2155 West Hwy. 89A, Suite 213, WS. 928-282-5560, 800-249-6875. www.jbjochum.com

Sedona Soul Adventures For more of a vision quest than just a rental, these folks offer a network of apartments, guest houses and homes for interested clients. They also offer to connect you with their network of healers and guides. 877-204-3664. www.sedonasouladventures.com

Camping

The major change in recent years has been the prohibition of freestyle camping through a large portion of the local forests. In exchange, the Forest Service has constructed a few new official campsites. Though it eliminates a bit of freedom, it helps prevent further damage to the forest.

For more nature and less civilization, I like Pine Flats, which is far up into the canyon. Here a spring of tasty clean water flows just to the side of the road, and you can nestle on pine needles under the tall ponderosas. Campground cost is $15 per night. Although all developed campgrounds are excluded from the Red Rock Pass, a separate site fee is required (see "Parks and Passes" for details). Call the Ranger Station at 928-282-4119 or stop by the South Gateway Visitor Center for details. Note that the old Ranger Station on Brewer Road has closed. For reservations (recommended), call the National Recreation Reservation Services at 877-444-6777.

CAMPSITES

	SEASON	# SITES	WATER	TOILETS	SHOWERS	RESERVATIONS	TRAILERS
Bootlegger							
	Apr 15-Oct 31	10	no	no	no	no	no
Cave Springs							
	Apr 15-Oct 31	82	yes	yes	yes	yes	yes, to 36 ft.
Chavez Crossing							
	All year	3 group	yes	yes	no	yes	yes, to 40 ft.
Manzanita							
	All year	18	yes	no	no	no	no
Pine Flats							
	Mar 1-Nov 15	57	yes	yes	no	yes	yes, to 36 ft.
Beaver Creek							
	All year	13	yes	yes	no	no	yes, to 22 ft.

Note that Banjo Bill along Oak Creek is no longer an overnight campground. For further information, write Coconino National Forest, Sedona Ranger District, P.O. Box 300, Sedona, AZ 86339-0300. www.redrockcountry.org

If you were hoping to escape even these signs of civilization, then you can head in one of three directions for dispersed camping. South, you can camp in the Beaver Creek area of I-17. North, go beyond the Oak Creek Vista and camp off Hwy 89A. East, you can camp between I-17 and Schnebly Hill Vista.

CAMPING SUPPLIES

Canyon Outfitters You'll find a nice collection of tents and backpacks upstairs, as well as cookware, water filters, shoes, clothing, headlamps and books on the first floor. 2701 W Hwy 89A, WS. 928-282-5293.

Sedona Sports Look for good gear and great camping advice here, including backpacks, water purification equipment, mess kits, and the best selection of hiking boots. Creekside Plaza, across from Tlaquepaque, 251 Hwy 179. 928-282-1317. www.sedonasports.com

Timeshares

Wanna buy a week? Sedona's offerings are abundant. Here they are in alphabetical order.

RESORTS AND FRACTIONAL OWNERSHIP COMMUNITIES

Hyatt Piñon Pointe New, and in the heart of Uptown. Great views, especially from the pool. One-bedroom, two-bedroom and studios, including fireplaces and private terraces. 1 N Hwy 89A, at the "Y." 928-204-8820, 800-926-4447.

Fairfield Resorts Spacious and well-located. 2445 W Hwy 89A, Suite 2, WS. 928-203-9744, 800-834-6898.

Los Abrigados Perhaps the most amenities of any site, with a health club and spa, pools, tennis courts, miniature golf and a bocce court. There is access to Oak Creek, and next door is the charming Tlaquepaque shopping galleria. 160 Portal Lane, BTY. 928-204-1520, 800-521-3131.

Sedona Pines 6701 W Hwy 89A. 928-282-6640, 800-547-8727.

Seven Canyons Beyond upscale is ultra-scale with red rock views and an 18-hole Tom Weiskopf golf course. Offering estate lots, fractional ownership villas and private golf memberships. 3755 Long Canyon Road, WS. 928-203-2000, 866-367-8844.

Sunterra Corporation Includes "The Ridge," timeshares on the edge of the Sedona Golf Resort. Corporate office: 401 Jordan Road, Suite A, UP. 928-204-9481, 888-447-2767.

TIMESHARE RESALE BROKERS

Go Timeshare 204 Hwy 179, BTY. 928-204-2222, 877-208-2224.
Timeshare Resale Brokers, Inc. 431 Hwy 179, Suite 5, BTY. 928-203-0777, 800-670-9707.

3

Exploring Sedona's Wonders

The Top 14 Sites

This wouldn't be a tourist destination without places to see, and Sedona has some of the world's prettiest. The following list provides a taste of Sedona's natural beauty and good energy, with splashes of ancient history and local culture added. Note that getting from one place to another almost always requires a car, as the spots range across the town and the surrounding forest.

41

If you're really pressed for time, you can pick Bell Rock, Cathedral Rock, the Chapel of the Holy Cross, Tlaquepaque and Airport Mesa. All deserve longer, but with 10 minutes at each stop you could do this short tour in about two hours.

To see all of them in a day seems a little crazy to me, but if you insist on the "Been There, Done That" T-shirt, here are a few tips. Remember that Sedona is large: From Slide Rock in the Oak Creek Canyon to Palatki at the end of dirt road west of town could take as much as an hour. Second, Palatki requires a reservation: If you've only got today, call Palatki first. Third, consider mobility. The Seven Sacred Pools and Palatki require some walking, and in fact all sites can be better appreciated by getting out of the car.

If your primary interest is our famous vortex energy, then avoid playing Vortex Roulette. Tourists with too little time race among Boynton Canyon, Cathedral Rock, Bell Rock and Airport Mesa. Yes, there's energy here for sure, but you won't find an "X" that marks the spot. Besides, speeding from one to another defeats the purpose of finding a place that will take you deeper. Instead, pull over somewhere, any-where, and walk on the red earth itself. If you just can't leave with-out "standing on a vortex," then go to one that draws you, and stay long enough to remember it. If you do, you may understand why locals boast that "God made the Grand Canyon but lives in Sedona."

(($)) **7-Day Red Rock Pass** One of the hottest deals in town is the weekly pass. It now includes new areas that you'd otherwise have to pay for, even with a day pass.

AIRPORT MESA

What You'll See

High above West Sedona, you'll have a splendid view of its rock formations and the town below.

How to Get There

Head west 1.1 miles on Hwy 89A from the "Y." Turn left onto Airport Road and continue up to the top of the mesa. Park to the left in the gravel lot, and walk across to the overlook. Some folks choose to park at a dirt pullout on the left on the way up, which also offers nice views with a bit of climbing.

The Scoop

While Sedona's average altitude is 4,500 feet above sea level, there's nothing average about it! Here, you stand at nearly 5,000 feet, looking across to Capitol Butte (aka: Thunder Mountain) at over 6,500 feet. Follow its profile to the right and you'll make out the spout of Coffee Pot rock at the end of the ridge line. Sugarloaf is the lumpy hill below and back to the left. North and east is Wilson Mountain at 7,122 feet, the town's tallest formation, coated with a chocolate-gray basalt rock from a lava flow millions of years ago.

Senator John McCain owns a home west of Sedona and used this spot to give a press conference at the end of his run for the presidency in 2000. Snow had fallen the night before, and it shimmered that spring morning under blue skies and brilliant sunshine. The mass of reporters and well-wishers who followed McCain's campaign scrambled for parking on what was then a field. The snow turned the dirt to mud, and more than one news team truck was hopelessly stuck. The popularity of this overlook led the town to gravel the area, creating the parking lot you'll use here.

Keep In Mind

It gets crowded here at sunset, especially on weekend nights. On the return, it's tough to make a left onto Hwy 89A. You might try a right, then turn around at Real Estate Central or the pullout further down along the north side of the highway.

CHAPEL OF THE HOLY CROSS

What You'll See

Sedona's most sacred building is fascinating architecture.

How to Get There

Head north three miles from Bell Rock or south from the "Y" for four miles. Look for Chapel Road to the left if you're coming from Uptown or to the right if you're coming from the Village of Oak Creek. Follow Chapel Road all the way to the building. I recommend pulling over below for a photo, but save yourself a very long walk by continuing uphill. The church is reached via a steep but smooth concrete ramp. A wheelchair is sometimes available at its base if you or a fellow passenger is physically challenged, but it will take quite a bit of pushing to get to the top.

The Scoop

As a young woman in New York City, Margaret Staude noticed a cross in the gridirons of the Empire State Building. If skyscrapers represented modern commerce, wasn't it also time for a church that would speak to modern spirituality? Inspired to create that church, she worked on the idea with her friend, Lloyd Wright, son of architect Frank Lloyd Wright. Although she had looked across America and Europe for a spot, the dream was realized when—while vacationing here—she noticed a pillar formation to the east of the present church. The Chapel of the Holy Cross was completed in 1954. Look east (to your left as you face the Chapel's door, or right as you face the cross) and count past the first two chunky pillars. You'll notice a gap, and then a narrow pillar that Marguerite thought looked just like the "Madonna and Child." See it? The two chunkier pillars are known as The Nuns.

Keep In Mind

This is perhaps Sedona's single most visited spot. Crowds start showing up about two hours after Phoenix finishes breakfast. The chief difficulty if you've arrived on a weekend is making a left turn onto Hwy 179. That can be done a little more easily if you cut through the Lutheran Church parking on the left at the intersection. Closed on Easter, Christmas and New Year's Day. 780 Chapel Road, 928-282-4069.

44

TLAQUEPAQUE

What You'll See

Sedona's loveliest shopping galleria offers Spanish colonial architecture, towering sycamores, pretty porticos, fountains and open spaces.

The Scoop

In the 1970s entrepreneur Abe Miller had a vision to build an artist colony fashioned after a Mexican village of the same name. He found the perfect location on the banks of Oak Creek, shaded by tall sycamores. Today, with its arched entries and cobblestone walkways, Tlaquepaque (Tlah-keh-pah-keh) conveys a sense of timelessness that feels more like three centuries than three decades.

A wide variety of art is represented by more than 40 galleries and specialty shops. Yet even non-shoppers will find the setting delightful. Colorful flowers and vine-covered walls could inspire a photo essay or an afternoon siesta while your partner shops away. Round a corner and you may see a wedding in progress at the quaint chapel, hear a musician playing, watch a sculptor at work, or meet an author at a book signing.

Exquisite landscaping helps Tlaquepaque reflect the seasons. The lush sycamores provide summer shade and foliage in the autumn. By the time their leaves drop, the lighting of the luminarias (a Southwestern holiday tradition) is upon us.

Keep In Mind

Shops are open 10am to 5pm every day except Thanksgiving and Christmas. Hours vary for the four restaurants, which include the Oak Creek Brewery and René. Parking can become crowded on weekends.

Among the events held here during the year are "Shakespeare in Sedona" in June and July; festivals and art events in spring and autumn; and the lighting of luminarias in December.

BELL ROCK

What You'll See

This red rock welcomes you as you approach Sedona, and is fun to scamper around.

How to Get There

If coming from Phoenix, you'll see Bell Rock on the right as you pass through the southern side of town, known as the Village of Oak Creek. If you're coming from Uptown or the "Y," follow Hwy 179 south for seven miles. Park on the left or right, but take caution if you are crossing the road. Visiting drivers often watch the red rocks more than the streets. For a one-mile hike to the rock, park at the Bell Rock Pathway Vista Parking Lot, just north of the Circle K convenience store on the east side of Hwy 179.

The Scoop

People of all ages find Bell Rock cool. It's so big on the one hand, and yet so easy to reach on the other. This is a perfect example of why Sedona can be considered the opposite of its geological big brother, the Grand Canyon. The modern history of human visitors to that canyon shows people constantly underestimating its vast size. The first Europeans to see it thought it to be a few miles across, when in fact it is more than a dozen. Now look at Bell Rock: It wouldn't be shocking to wonder, at first, how many hours (or even days) it would take to climb it. Look closer and you'll see people on the higher portions who have made it there in a matter of minutes. Look behind Bell Rock and you'll see the impressive monolith known as Courthouse Butte. A trail encircles Bell Rock and Courthouse, although there is no path between them.

Keep In Mind

Sadly, there are at least two easy ways to get hurt here. The first is trying to reach the very top. Believe me, we've rescued enough people already: Settle for pretty close to the top. Second, flat soles on these gritty dirt-covered rocks are a disaster. Play it safe. On downhill portions, turn your feet to the side, and sidestep down the steep parts. (Even better, get a pair of good shoes at Sedona Sports, across the street and just uphill from Tlaquepaque and Los Abrigados.)

CATHEDRAL ROCK

What You'll See

This is Sedona's most famous and most impressive formation.

How to Get There

This can be tricky because the best views of Cathedral Rock are actually at a distance. To get to the formation itself, travel on Hwy 179 south of the "Y" for about four miles, turning right onto Back O' Beyond Road. After a half-mile of narrow curves, you'll see a parking lot on the left, placing you at the foot of the formation.

The Scoop

The gentle choice here is just to enjoy the view as you drive to Cathedral Rock, or admire it from the parking lot. It takes a bit of effort to hike up the lower third of the mountain from here, bringing you to a nice flat ridge. For the big climb, continue to the right from that ridge, looking for the cairn that marks the start of a steep ascent. This can be done without technical gear but shouldn't be attempted if you've got any body parts that hurt.

Believe it or not, this rock was long ago misnamed when a mapmaker transposed its original name, Courthouse, with the butte next to Bell Rock.

Keep In Mind

If you haven't been climbing lately, then you need to know right now that coming down is actually harder than going up—perhaps not as strenuous, but definitely more anxiety producing. So—on the steep portions, you might want to stop, turn around, and try on the downhill step for size. No problem? Then you're set to continue higher. For sunset watchers, remember also that there are no inlaid footlights to escort you back. Make sure to return as soon as the sun drops, if not sooner.

RED ROCK CROSSING

What You'll See

Here you'll find views of Sedona's most famous and most impressive formation, from the prettiest spot.

How to Get There

The best views of Cathedral Rock are actually at a distance. Drive west from Sedona on Hwy 89A. Turn left onto Upper Red Rock Loop Road, which curves downward. Take the first left-hand turn onto Chavez Ranch Road. Chavez will lead to Crescent Moon Ranch, an official park. From the Village of Oak Creek, take Verde Valley School Road. It intersects Hwy 179 at a stoplight south of the outlet mall, and north of the Hilton entrance. Follow it all the way. It becomes a dirt road that is okay for passenger cars. The parking lot is on the left a hundred yards from the creek. You can walk the road to the best-known photo spot, or follow the trail across from the parking lot for a nice walk.

NO

The Scoop

Along gentle Oak Creek, stately cottonwoods and Arizona sycamores create a unique combination: red rocks, flowing water and autumn foliage. Whether you're in time for the foliage or not (November is best), it is always pretty here. In spring and summer, the greenery adds lushness to the high desert reds, while in winter the fallen leaves clear the way for views of the deep blue sky. At Crescent Moon Ranch, a cement sidewalk parallels the creek, and walking possibilities continue even after it ends. Environmental toilets are available. On the Verde Valley School Road side, there are lots of red rocks to prance around on.

Keep In Mind

Hours at Crescent Moon Ranch are 8am to 8pm from Memorial Day through Labor Day, 8am to dusk the rest of the year. Parking there costs $7, but is now included with the one-week Red Rock Pass. Parking at Verde Valley School Road is free. There is no vehicular crossing over the creek.

BOYNTON CANYON

What You'll See
This splendid Sedona canyon hosts world-class Enchantment Resort.

How to Get There
From the "Y," head west on Hwy 89A for three miles. Turn right at the stoplight and follow Dry Creek Road for 2.8 miles to the stop sign then turn left onto FR 152C, also called Boynton Pass Road. Follow this road for 1.5 miles to a stop sign. Go right for 0.1 mile to the parking lot on the right. This is the trail entrance.

The Scoop
The hiking trail continues a full three miles deep into the canyon. Just outside the entrance to the resort, you'll notice a pillar that appears to have a boulder glued on top of it. This is Kachina Woman, the source of the Yavapai creation myth. According to one version of the legend, a great flood filled the land, destroying the people. One young woman was rescued by a mythical woodpecker, and together they procreated the tribe anew.

Keep In Mind
Enchantment Resort generally does not allow visitors to take a look around: You'll be politely asked to turn around at the gate house entry. Calling ahead for a reservation at the restaurant or grill, however, is a way to get the view and a meal too. The Boynton Canyon Trail is open to the public, and from it, you can walk closer to Kachina Woman, via the Vista Trail.

SEVEN SACRED POOLS

What You'll See
Soldiers Pass Trail reveals a tall formation, small pools of water and a deep sinkhole.

How to Get There

From the "Y," travel west on Hwy 89A a little over a mile, turning right at the stoplight. Follow Soldiers Pass Road for less than three miles, turning right onto Rim Shadows. This bit is tricky, but follow it ahead through a curvy intersection, and look for the narrow gated entry to the parking lot on the left.

The Scoop
Start by the trail kiosk to the right, rather than the jeep road to the left. A 25-minute hike of moderate difficulty will show you three interesting geological formations. Five minutes ahead, turn left as you reach a cairn or rock pile wrapped in mesh. A right turn leads to Jordan Trail. Just beyond the cairn and sign is Devil's Kitchen, a large sinkhole that appeared sometime in the 1890s. All of it, that is, except for the large chunk of stone lodged in the back. Grand Piano Rock fell almost a hundred years later. Above towers the interesting formation known as the Sphinx.

Follow the path up to the left (west) around the sinkhole and stay on the narrow walking trail. Seven more minutes of walking brings you to a spot that was given the name Seven Sacred Pools by a jeep driver who is known to spend time in Hawaii. I'm recommending a new name, not to diminish them, but to put them in proper perspective—Seven Sacred Puddles. Stepping across to the red rock ridge brings you to the jeep road, which you can follow back.

Keep In Mind
The presence of a jeep company tour means you may not have the spot all to yourself. Also be aware of mountain bikers coming around curves. Or, if you're the mountain biker, keep your eye out for walkers. Hikers have the right-of-way over bikers, and riders on horseback trump both.

SCHNEBLY HILL

What You'll See
This rough and rocky historic road reveals awesome scenic views.

How to Get There

Head south from the "Y" for less than a half-mile, getting into the narrow left-hand turn lane just over the bridge. If you are coming up Hwy 179 from the south, bear right to join Schnebly Hill Road instead of crossing the bridge. You can play it safe and park at the lot on the left as the pavement ends, or go higher on the rough dirt road. If so, park at pullouts rather than in the road. A hiking trail, the Munds Wagon Trail, parallels the road for much of the route.

The Scoop
This road is named for Sedona's first family, the Schneblys, who had a farm and hosted travelers. In 1902 townspeople developed this cattle trail into a road in order to create a better route to Flagstaff.

Highlights include Snoopy Rock, best viewed from the paved road, about one-fifth mile below the parking lot. Look south and you'll see a tall formation. Follow the sheer right edge of the rock to find Snoopy. He is lying on his dog house, and you'll see the outline of his nose, belly and feet, looking from left to right.

Red rock formations include the long, narrow Moose Ridge, Giant's Thumb and Tea Pot Rock. The Cow Pies Trail begins across from the rocky lot three miles up the road, and Merry Go Round Rock is another mile higher. The road continues for a long, rough nine miles. It can also be snowy or muddy in the high country. However, if you make it, you can reconnect with I-17 to return.

Keep In Mind
When we say bumpy, we mean it. Best car to drive this in: someone else's. Even better, someone else's SUV. Beware of oncoming drivers who drive where the road is smoother, rather than on their side. Also keep an eye out for protruding rocks that can bust an oil pan or shred a sidewall. If you're here for sunset, take care to avoid the side of the road in the darkness as you return. The edges can drop steeply.

SLIDE ROCK

What You'll See
Oak Creek creates a natural flume for swimmers.

How to Get There
From Uptown, drive seven miles north on Hwy 89A. The park is on the left-hand side.

The Scoop
To the north rests the Colorado Plateau. To the south lies the Sonoran Desert. In between? Sedona. Here at Slide Rock you'll see that the slow but awesome movements of geology between these two land masses has resulted in a playful place in nature.

Check out the old farm machinery in one of the area's original apple orchards, or follow a path further up the creekside. Here, you'll see the tall green trees that bless Sedona and Flagstaff with shared responsibility for the largest ponderosa pine forest in the world. Walking to the creek, take a look in at Slide Rock Market for local goods, including apples. At the creek itself, walk carefully. Dry rock is trustworthy, wet rock is not, and icy rock in winter is treacherous.

Keep In Mind
Slide Rock is very, very crowded on summer days as Arizonans seek to beat the heat. If you find the wait at the parking lot is too long for your taste, you can head further north to dine at Junipine Café and walk at West Fork. Alternatively, return south and shop at Garland's Indian Store or seek a tasty sandwich at the market next door. Occasionally, swimming or wading at Slide Rock is restricted according to water quality. The park entry fee is $8 normally, but $10 in summer and without an attendant to give you change.

RED ROCK LOOP ROAD

What You'll See
This scenic drive shows off views of beautiful Cathedral Rock and the Mogollon Rim.

How to Get There
Head west on Hwy 89A four miles from the "Y." Turn left at the intersection. The stoplight and Red Rock High School serve as your landmarks.

The Scoop
This route on the west side of Sedona offers tremendous scenes featuring the town's most impressive formations. If you begin at Upper Red Rock Loop Road, you'll first notice Red Rock High School on the right. Several pullouts are available on the left-hand side as you drop into the valley. Pick one, get out and enjoy the views. The most impressive formation in the distance is Cathedral Rock. Courthouse Butte is the monolith to its left. Looking to the east, you'll see Arizona's portion of the Colorado Plateau, known as the Mogollon (MUH-gee-on) Rim. Notice the smooth upward incline of Airport Mesa, northeast in the distance, and you may see a plane take off.

You can choose to turn left at the first opportunity, onto Chavez Ranch Road. This winding road will lead you to Crescent Moon Ranch, located on the left just before Chavez Ranch Road ends. Otherwise, Upper Red Rock Loop Road will turn to a gravel road, which winds past Red Rock State Park. Easy trails and an informative visitor center await here. Continue as the gravel again becomes pavement and you'll eventually return to Hwy 89A, less than two miles west of where you left it. Turn right onto Hwy 89A to complete the loop.

Keep In Mind
If you go at sunset, note that it may be very dark on the drive back. Use caution on the curves.

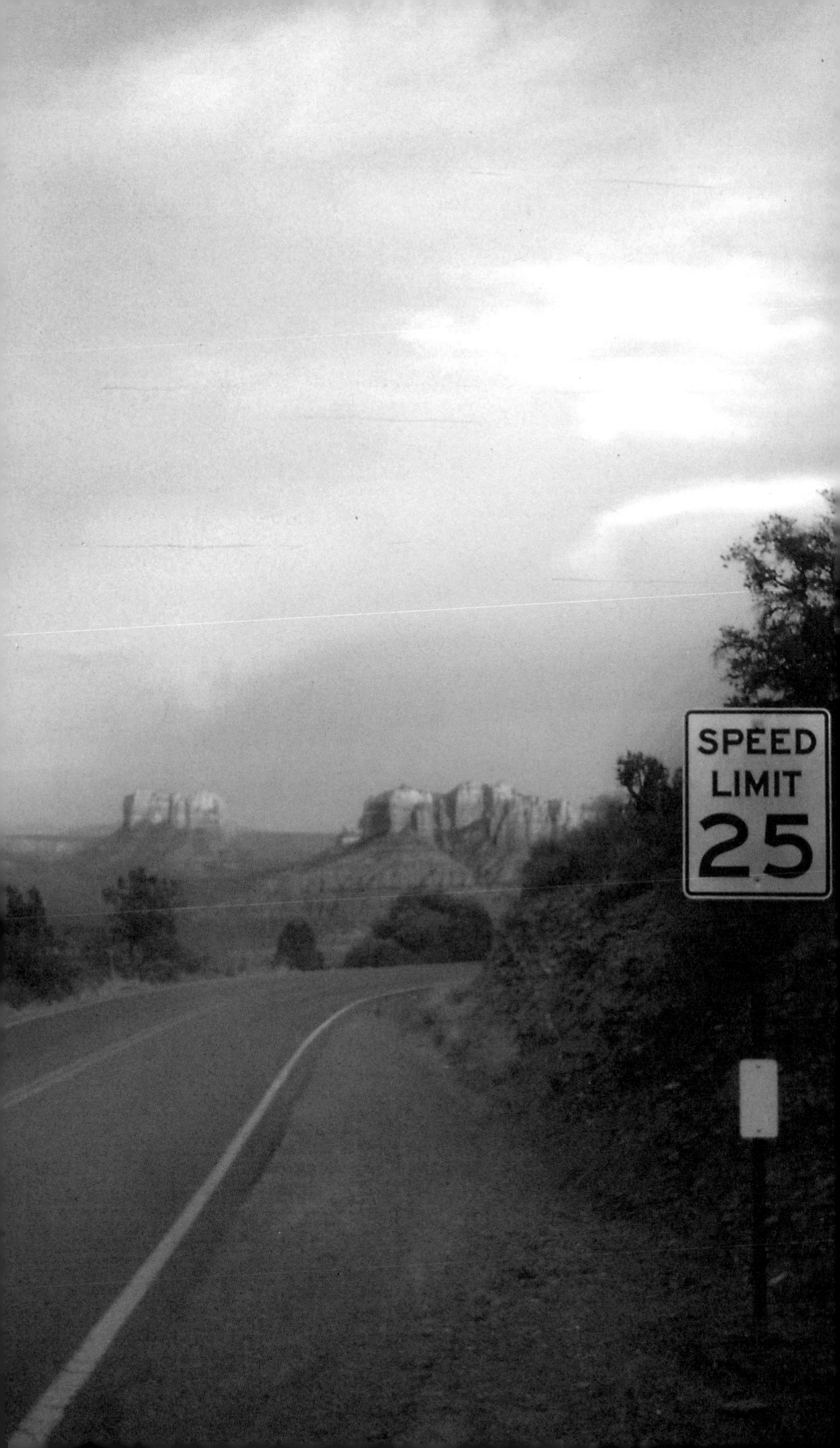
SPEED
LIMIT
25

MIDGLEY BRIDGE

What You'll See
An easy pull-off just past Uptown reveals Wilson Mountain above and Oak Creek below.

How to Get There

Head north of Uptown less than a mile on Hwy 89A. Slow as you cross the bridge, and park in the lot to the left. Pull in close to allow other visitors to enter.

The Scoop
Once you park, get out and take a look at Wilson Mountain, Sedona's tallest formation. On its upper portions, notice that the soil appears a dark gray color. Evidence suggests that volcanic activity in this area millions of years ago laid down a layer of lava here. Hardening with time, lava becomes basalt, a craggy, tough rock that doesn't wear away with the ease of Sedona sandstone. If you'd like to walk from here, follow signs for Jim Thompson Trail or Wilson Canyon. Both are gentle-to-moderate walks, and there may be signs of water in the dry creek bed. Climbing Wilson takes no technical gear, just good hiking boots. But the round-trip is a five-hour effort or more, and should be done with food, water and enough time to beat the sunset.

Stairs lead down below the bridge where you can see the leafy trees (cottonwoods and Arizona sycamores) below, as well as The Beach, the red rock shore where teens hit the water in summer. You can follow the trail under the bridge to the overlook. Above to the left are the red rocks of the Schnebly Hill area. Below is Oak Creek, and if you don't already know the season, the leaves on the trees will tell you. Now shift your eyes to the cliff behind and imagine what it is like to climb down to get to The Beach.

Keep In Mind
The small parking area at the bridge crowds quickly. Sometimes you can find a spot by looking in deeper, closer to the trailhead. Wherever you park, be considerate by pulling in head-on.

SNOOPY ROCK

What You'll See

Look for a formation with an uncanny resemblance to the Peanuts character.

How to Get There

View Snoopy from the east side of the main street in Uptown, between Uptown and the "Y," or a mile along the paved portion of Schnebly Hill Road.

The Scoop

Here's how to see it. Look for the large, tall formation wedged between the Schnebly Hill Road and the Mogollon Rim along the east side of town. Focus on the sheer cliff edge to the right. As you follow it down, your eye will come upon the back of Snoopy's head. Snoopy is lying on his doghouse, so his snout, then belly and feet are all pointing up. Snoopy is in many ways the prime Rorschach test for the red rocks. Just as psychologists use ink blots to understand what you see, Sedonans use Snoopy to test your imagination. From here, you can move on to find all kinds of features in the rocks that appear and disappear with the changes of light through the day and the seasons.

Keep In Mind

Charles Schultz, the Peanuts creator, died a few years ago, but Snoopy has been here for eons. Ideally, don't be looking for Snoopy if you're the one driving!

PALATKI

What You'll See
These wonderful Indian ruins are nearly a thousand years old, and the cliffs nearby feature pictographs and petroglyphs.

How to Get There
These rough dirt roads are best for your SUV or somebody else's rental car. From the "Y," head three miles west to the light at Dry Creek Road. Turn right (north). At the "T" where the road ends, turn left (no sign, but it is known as Boynton Pass Road), following signs for Enchantment Resort. A couple of miles ahead, turn left at the stop sign. (Believe it or not, this is also Boynton Pass Road.) Continue for about four miles (it will seem like 10 due to the dirt road). Turn right onto FR 795, following signs for Palatki. It is less than two miles to the parking lot. You can drive on more pavement and somewhat smoother dirt if you instead follow 89A west through and out of town. About three-quarters of a mile south of milepost 365, look for the mailboxes and turn right onto FR 525. It is eight miles to the parking lot.

The Scoop
This Sedona treasure is the ultimate expression of the area's ancient past. The Sinagua lived here nearly a millenium ago, though the site has been used by Native groups from twelve thousand years ago to pioneer times. From the host cabin, a one-third mile dirt trail reaches two-story adobe ruins plugged under red rock cliffsides. In a different direction, another trail leads to rock art, some etched, some painted onto the cliff walls. Don't quit looking until you find the Kokopelli, the horseman and the bears.

Keep In Mind
The trails are not difficult, but they are not accessible for those in wheelchairs. Don't trust other guide books: A reservation is now mandatory to visit Palatki. Call 928-282-3854 on any day to make one, 9:30am-3pm. Winter precipitation doesn't come often, but when it does, it can cause the closure of the dirt roads leading to Palatki. Signs indicating the closed status will normally be posted on Boynton Pass Road. Hours are 9:30am-3:30pm, seven days a week.

Itineraries

MAKING THE MOST OF A DAY

Suppose you've got only a day in Sedona. You've got a lot to do today, so start early. Grab breakfast at the Coffee Pot Restaurant or get your coffee fix at Ravenheart. At either place, you are surrounded by locals and visitors who know what's going on and who can give you more advice.

The smart visitor knows the best stuff in town is outdoors, so pick up some water and supplies as preparation for your adventure. Choose from Bell Rock Pathway for an easy hike, Boynton Canyon for something moderate, or Bear Mountain for the extreme. (See "Hikes" for details.) If you want something even gentler, try Red Rock State Park. Instead, you could rest your feet and have nature brought to you on a Pink Jeep Tour. I recommend Broken Arrow, their signature outing.

Spend lunchtime in Uptown, taking time to stroll the promenade. Hungry? The best sandwiches are at Sedona Memories Bakery Café. Insiders call ahead (928-282-0032) to avoid waiting in line, and to receive the free cookie with every phone order.

In the afternoon, head north to drive through lovely Oak Creek Canyon, choosing Rainbow Trout Farm, Slide Rock State Park or West Fork Trail to experience it at its best. As an alternative, visit the Chapel of the Holy Cross for fantastic views and spiritual uplift, then head to Tlaquepaque for some shopping. Head across the street if you'd like to have your fortune told at the Crystal Castle or the Center for the New Age. Wondering what a vortex is? You may not have time to figure it out, but you can try by visiting famous Bell Rock, off Hwy 179 in the Village of Oak Creek.

Take note of the sunset hour (see "Sunsets") and head up to Airport Mesa, stopping on top for views from the overlook. You can stay up here to dine at the Airport Restaurant as you watch the stars come out. Spend the last few minutes of your day making plans for a longer visit on your return!

MAKING THE MOST OF A WEEK

Suppose you have a week in Sedona. Well, at least now we have some quality time to work with! Let me congratulate you on making the wise choice to hang around. Take the following advice, and you'll see a Sedona that the two-hour tourists don't even know exists. Here are seven great days all planned out for you. Mix and match as you like.

First, spend a day on the trails. (Personally, I'd spend all seven days on the hiking trails.) Begin at New York Bagels & Donuts to pick up breakfast plus a sandwich for the trail. The choices listed under "Hiking" will give you some options. Other good trails include Doe Mountain and nearby Fay Canyon. If you prefer bike trails, then consult the experts. Sedona Bike & Bean is best for novices, close to the Bell Rock Pathway. Mountain Bike Heaven is best if you want big thrills. Rent one of their high-end demos, join a group ride, and you'll come back with stories and a nickname.

Second, enjoy a day in Oak Creek Canyon. Explore Garland's Native American Jewelry store and grab a sandwich in the market next door. Life in the canyon is all about Oak Creek, so you'll want to walk it or fish it. The West Fork Trail is historic, Slide Rock State Park scenic, and either can be complemented with lunch at Junipine Café. If you pick fishing instead, call Jim McInness of Gon' Fishen to guide you to the best fishing holes. You'll spend less time fishing but more time eating fish at Rainbow Trout Farm, which has grills to cook up what you harvest. At Indian Gardens, you can find juicy peaches in the summertime and hot cider in the autumn and winter.

Third, explore the fascinating remains of ancient civilizations. Palatki hosts Indian ruins plus petroglyphs and pictographs, and enough rangers and volunteers to explain the difference. If you are staying in the Village of Oak Creek, stick with the southern trio of glyphs at "V Bar V," ruins at Montezuma Castle and mysteries at Montezuma Well.

Fourth, moving from ancient art to modern, gallery hopping is well worth a day of your time. Take what I call the Sedona Art Walk. Begin at Hillside Plaza and visit galleries there, along Hwy 179, and then cross the bridge to see those in Tlaquepaque.

Fifth, gain an interesting perspective by spending a day on Sedona's architecture. I suggest an eclectic mix of the religious, the retail and the nouveau riche. Visit the Chapel of the Holy Cross for spiritual wonders, then head to Tlaquepaque to stroll among the fountains, arches and tile staircases of this re-creation of a Colonial Mexican town. Finish by driving up Jordan Road in Uptown to Jordan Park, where you can drive around some of Sedona's priciest real estate.

Sixth, allow one day for Sedona's tour companies to show you what you might not find on your own. In fact, A Day In The West has just the right offer, not to mention the right name. They'll combine a jeep ride, horseback ride and a cowboy cookout for you. If you're sticking to jeeps alone, then try a deeper experience with Earth Wisdom Tours to explore Sedona's mystical side. See it all from above with Sedona Sky Treks or Arizona Helicopter Adventures. You could also see it all from above in a dawn departure with Northern Light or Red Rock Balloon.

Seventh, you now have time to supplement Sedona with side trips. The Grand Canyon is two hours and fifteen minutes away via the direct route, but there's an extended route that shows you much more. (See the "Side Trips" chapter for details.) It's a full-day experience. A half-day is all you'll need for Jerome, the ghost town west of Sedona. It's 35 minutes away and well worth visiting.

Of course you're going to spend all seven days eating, but where? If you want to eat well but don't want to spend all the money on one meal, visit Sedona's Little Italy. With 10 places serving some form of Italian cuisine on the west side of town, you'll have plenty of choices. A Pizza Heaven, Picazzo's and Troia's offer very good pasta and pizza at moderate prices in a nice atmosphere. Nearby Dahl & DiLuca is a step up in style and quality.

You know about Airport Mesa for the sunset: Now try places like Red Rock Crossing, Snoopy Rock and Lee Mountain. Insiders know that Sedona's sunsets are not best in the west, but to the east, where the setting sun turns the red rocks a glowing orange. Spend other evenings trying to find your own sunset spot. At night, remember to celebrate your good fortune. There's bound to be something happening this week at Casa Rincon.

Feel as if you need a vacation from your vacation? Finish restfully with a massage at Red Rock Healing Arts, and then listen to Jesse Kalu play the flute at Sedona Pines Resort.

73

Need a Restroom?

There's one to cover you in almost any part of town.

In **Oak Creek Canyon**, try out back of the deli/general store next to Garland's jewelry store. On the west side of Sedona, stop in at the Giant gas station on Hwy 89A. In Uptown, there's a loo next to the Chamber of Commerce on the southwest side of the street. In the Village of Oak Creek, the Outlet Mall is reliable. Aim for the passage between The Marketplace Café and Taco Bell in the mall's southeast corner.

If you're out near Enchantment Resort but can't get in, or you're coming back from Palatki without a toilet in sight, you can stop in at the **Boynton Canyon trailhead** parking lot for the toilet there.

Driving up from or down to Phoenix? Even if you don't need to go, the place to stop just in case is **Sunset Point**. It's exactly halfway there (or here).

Scenic Drives

Whether you like your drives smooth or rough, Sedona's scenery can make taking one very enjoyable. At all stops along the way, you should signal clearly and slow down gradually to alert drivers following, some of whom may be watching the scenery more closely than the road. How long your drive takes depends on how fast you drive and how often you stop, but plan a minimum of 90 minutes to complete any of them. Remember that no off-road driving is allowed in the Coconino National Forest.

SMOOTH ROUTES

HIGHWAY 89A, OAK CREEK CANYON

My first recommendation for a drive is to cover whichever portion of the route you didn't see on your way here. Hwy 89A qualifies as a scenic route after exiting I-17 on your way into town from Phoenix, and continuing through Uptown Sedona for a dozen miles though Oak Creek Canyon. Little advice is required to make the most of this enjoyable drive through Oak Creek Canyon. Driving north from Uptown, head over Midgley Bridge and turn sharply left into the parking lot at the base of Wilson Mountain. I recommend walking under the bridge to find a lookout point that offers a view above the creek. To get closer to the creek, you might stop less than a mile ahead on the right-hand side of Hwy 89A at Grasshopper Point. The winding road takes you down to the creekside, where the Allen's Bend Trail is a gentle half-mile that is easy to follow. The Rainbow Trout Farm is a bit ahead, also on the right-hand side. Not only can you catch fish at the farm, but they've also got grills for you to cook them on.

It just gets better as you continue north on Hwy 89A, with stops such as Garland's, known for its wonderful Indian jewelry collection, and Slide Rock State Park. You can walk by the creek, take a dip yourself, or have some apple cider at Slide Rock Market. The highway winds along the creek through both evergreen and deciduous trees that grow in the shadow of tall sandstone walls. Continue on to the café at Junipine Resort to have a meal. Eleven miles from Uptown is West Fork, on the left-hand side of the road. This historic and scenic spot, with a picnic area and 3-mile (one way) trail, was made famous by writer Zane Grey. His book *Call of the Canyon* described the beauty of the autumn leaves in this part of the canyon. I recommend turning around soon after passing West Fork. Otherwise, you can continue up the switchbacks, climbing over 1,000 feet to the Colorado Plateau.

SOUTH, OFF OF HWY 89A
RED ROCK LOOP ROAD

In contrast to narrow Oak Creek Canyon, Red Rock Loop Road offers big, juicy views, beginning off Hwy 89A, about four miles from the center of Sedona. There's a stoplight at the intersection, with the Zaki Gordon Film Institute on the right. Turn left onto Upper Red Rock Loop Road, and you'll first pass Sedona Red Rock High School on the right. As the road begins its winding descent, you'll see a number of left-hand pullouts for picture taking. Take a left turn onto Chavez Ranch Road. Follow the winding, paved road a couple of minutes until you see the Crescent Moon Park entrance on the left.

If you walk along the creek here, you'll come to Red Rock Crossing, with a view of Cathedral Rock in the distance. It is one of the prettiest spots you'll ever find. Retrace the drive to the Loop Road, heading uphill if you want to return on smooth pavement. To continue on, turn left and don't worry about the change to gravel. It doesn't get too rough if you drive carefully. Eventually, after the road returns to pavement, you'll see the entrance to Red Rock State Park. It's a few dollars to enter, and your Red Rock Pass does not cover the entrance fee. The park is home to numerous gentle trails and picnic spots, as well as a visitor center. To finish this extended loop, turn left after exiting the park onto what is here called Lower Red Rock Loop Road, which will eventually return you to Hwy 89A. A right-hand turn onto Hwy 89A will bring you back to town.

ROUGH ROUTES

SCHNEBLY HILL ROAD

Schnebly Hill Road is centrally located, branching out from Hwy 179 as it crosses the creek, a third of a mile below the "Y." The road is not recommended for passenger cars, and you'll see why a mile ahead when it turns to rock. Last chance to turn around on the pavement is at the Marg's Draw/Huckaby Trailhead parking lot on the left, and there's a toilet here too. Sedonans built this road in 1902 to bring their produce to market in Flagstaff. One stop along the way is the giant red sandstone slab that serves as a parking lot for the Cow Pies Trail across the road. If instead you continue driving, the zigzag route continues to climb, and the view improves all the way. Another pullout comes at Merry-Go-Round, a red rock formation wrapped by a belt of pink-white stone known as the Fort Apache layer. If you've come this far, don't turn around before going a few hundred yards farther ahead, where northern views are revealed, including basalt-topped Wilson Mountain. This is a good place to turn around, unless you want to continue another 10 miles across the plateau to eventually rejoin I-17. If so, head south on I-17 and take the exit for Sedona for a very long loop.

ROBBER'S ROOST

Farther out of town is the trip to Robber's Roost, a cool spot that few people know about. Drive 9 miles west from the center of Sedona on Hwy 89A and keep your eyes open for Red Canyon Road, labeled FR 525 by the Forest Service. Out here there are cattle drives up to the high country each summer. This is rough road, which you'll follow 2.8 miles before turning left onto FR 525C. Continue on FR 525C for 6.8 miles, watching for FR 9530 on the left. You can follow FR 9530 for just over a mile to park by a seldom-hiked trail, which drops down and then climbs up to this red rock formation. Stay to the left as the trail climbs the hill and you'll wind around the north face of the mound. Following along the narrow side of the mound, you'll eventually begin to see the cave where horse thieves once hung out. The rounded-out cave wall is a popular image on postcards in town. Please respect this special spot and do no damage. From your parking spot, the hike takes under 15 minutes.

EXTENDED SCENIC DRIVES

OAK CREEK CANYON

Heading north on Hwy 89A brings you to the place that put Sedona on the map: Oak Creek Canyon. Stops on the way include Midgley Bridge, which offers a small parking lot and a scenic overlook. Wilson Mountain rises above. Over the next 13 miles you'll drive parallel to the creek and rise into a ponderosa pine forest. Both the creek and the cliffs are scenic. You'll pass shops selling Indian goods, famous Slide Rock park, the Junipine Resort and West Fork Trail. This drive ends by winding up tight switchbacks that set you atop the Colorado Plateau. At the Oak Creek Canyon Vista on the right, Navajos offer their crafts. Although you are now beyond the colored rocks of Sedona, the vista offers views of the forested cliffs.

Directions: Drive north from Uptown on Hwy 89A. It is 26 miles from Uptown through the canyon and back. The road is paved. Winter hits the canyon harder than Sedona, but the highway is typically plowed quickly.

Time: Allow two to five hours to enjoy a canyon fling.

SYCAMORE–RED ROCK LOOP

This drive passes along colorful canyons and cliffs, with a number of side trips to see more. The Sterling Canyon Spur leads to two of the most spectacular rock formations in the area. Devil's Bridge and Vultee Arch trails are two potential hikes from this road. The Boynton Canyon spur leads to Enchantment Resort and another hiking trail. Further into the wilderness, Loy Butte offers gorgeous views, while the Sycamore Canyon spur takes you past Robber's Roost to Sycamore Pass, the gateway to the Sycamore Canyon Wilderness. Visit them all and you can call it a day, finishing with sunset views.

Directions: From the "Y," drive three miles west on Hwy 89A to Dry Creek Road. Turn right (north), turning left as the road ends at the intersection with Boynton Canyon Road. At the next stop sign, turn left on Boynton Pass Road, FR 152C. In less than four miles, FR 152C intersects FR 525. From here you can turn north (right) to the Loy Butte spur or south (left) to continue the drive. Four miles ahead, FR 525 intersects FR 525C (Sycamore Pass Road), to the

77

Sycamore Canyon spur, and 5 miles further to return to Sedona. Red Rock Loop Road on the right provides a route to Red Rock Crossing and the Oak Creek about a mile south of town. Without the added spur, the drive is about 23 miles long.

Time: Allow three to six hours to maximize the enjoyment.

DESERT CANYON SCENIC DRIVE

Heading south of Sedona, you'll find yourself back in what some may consider the northern edge of the vast Sonoran Desert. There are more red rock canyons, ancient lava flows, creekside greenery, old ranches, and very, very old Native American ruins. Walking trails and back roads are available on the way, as signs indicate. There are campgrounds and picnic areas at Wet Beaver Creek Crossing and along West Clear Creek. A dirt road offers a route to an undeveloped campground at the start of West Clear Creek Canyon. For a side trip, visit Montezuma's Well National Monument, home of pit-house dwellers and cliff-dwellers. Roadrunners, coyotes and javelinas inhabit these areas.

Directions: Drive south from Sedona on Hwy 179, heading under the interstate onto FR 618. This is a gravel road. Follow this road along the base of the Mogollon Rim 13 miles to General Crook Road (paved) and turn west (right) 9 miles back to I-17. FR 618 is graveled and suitable for passenger cars. State Road 260 is paved. As a loop, the route meanders 60 miles from Uptown Sedona.

Time: Allow three to five hours to appreciate this area.

4

Red Rock Activities

Airport and Air Tours

SEDONA AIRPORT

If you're interested in flying to Sedona yourself, a couple points are worth noting. Sedona's airport is set amidst tremendous beauty, but the short runway and high altitude make this a landing not to be taken for granted. At 4,500 feet, Sedona lies on the escarpment of the Colorado Plateau, known around here as the Mogollon Rim. There are spectacular views and wildlife, but 2,000 feet of clearance is required above the National Forest. The airport is home to airplanes and helicopters, both private flyers and tours. Airplane arrival and departure paths are next to each other at the same end of the runway. Therefore, when departing and after takeoff, stay left, away from landing traffic. The other side of the airport is designated for helicopters.

TOURIST FLIGHTS

Arizona Helicopter Adventures Prefer the maneuverability of a chopper? You'll be in a Bell Jet Ranger Helicopter with a pilot offering a discussion of what you're seeing, which includes ruins. 235 Air Terminal Drive, Suite 7. 928-282-0904, 800-282-5141.

Maverick Helicopters Known for their VIP Grand Canyon tours, this company now offers tours from Sedona. $69-599 per person. 928-282-2980, 888-261-4414. www.maverickhelicopter.com

Red Rock Biplanes These loud and proud Waco planes offer views from an open cockpit and a video of your tour. From $89 per person. 1225 Airport Road, #14, WS. 928-204-5939, 800-866-7433. www.sedonaairtours.com

Sedona Sky Treks This tour and charter service offers scenic tours of Sedona, Grand Canyon and Monument Valley. From $35 per person for 15 minutes. 235 Air Terminal Drive, WS. 928-282-6628, 928-282-7768. www.skytreks.com

Ancient Ruins

HONANKI This wonderful set of ruins is far quieter than Palatki but treacherous to drive to in the wrong vehicle. Your car may pay the price for your solitude. The rock art is a bit less accessible and less varied. I send folks here who want a more unique experience and who are willing to put their car through anything. Near to Palatki as the crow flies, Honanki is far away as the car drives. If you do make it, you'll generally have it to yourself (per Forest Service, you should be out by dusk). Note that stabilization and trail construction is in progress here.

Directions: Take Hwy 89A southwest of Sedona to FR 525. U.S. Forest Service, Sedona/Beaver Creek Ranger District, 928-282-4119. Currently the USFS website does not mention Honanki. For information, go to www.aztecfreenet.org

★ **PALATKI** This is one of Sedona's special secrets. I like it because you can find petroglyphs stretching back 12,000 years as well as wonderful ruins. Great photos can be taken of both, particularly the ruins, which are set within a sheltering red rock cliff. The Forest Service recommends allowing one to two hours to appreciate all that is here. Reservations are required. Call Palatki at (928) 282-3854 between 9:30am and 3:00pm. Reservations are available for 9:30, 11:30 and 1:30. The entrance gate is closed about a half-hour before the site itself closes. Hours: 9:30am to 3:30pm seven days a week (subject to weather conditions). If there has been rain or snow recently, it is recommended that you contact the South Gateway Visitor Center to learn the condition of the roads to Palatki Heritage Site. If the roads are impassable, Palatki Heritage Site will be closed; signs indicating the closed status will normally be posted at key access points. A Red Rock Pass (or equivalent) is required on all vehicles parked at our cultural sites. This pass can be purchased at the sites during normal hours of operation. No pets are allowed.

Directions: Take Hwy 89A south from the "Y" (away from Uptown). About 0.75 mile south of mile marker 365, turn right onto FR 525. This forest road shortly changes to gravel, then dirt, but it's passable for passenger cars when dry. Drive eight miles to the Palatki Heritage Site and the parking lot.

MONTEZUMA CASTLE This site is neither a castle nor connected to Montezuma, but everything other than the name is perfect at this national monument. One million annual visitors agree. These ruins are truly for cliff dwellers, set high above Beaver Creek. Below these ancient condos are a self-guided walking tour, bookstore and rangers available for questions. This is a nice option on the way back to Phoenix. Allow 35 minutes from Uptown Sedona, less from the Village of Oak Creek. The heaviest visitation occurs during the spring, while December and January are the slowest times of the year. The town of Camp Verde is approximately five miles away. Pets with a leash are okay.

Directions: Take I-17 south to exit 293 and drive four miles on passable gravel/dirt roads. 8am-5pm daily. National Park Service, 928-567-3322. $3 per adult, 16 and younger free. www.nps.gov/moca/home.htm

TUZIGOOT Built on a hillside by the Sinagua around A.D. 1000, this pueblo included more than a hundred rooms. While most of the remains lack tall walls or a ceiling, the views go on for miles. Allow 35 minutes from Uptown Sedona. Open daily. Summer 8am-7pm. Winter 8am-5pm. Closed on Christmas Day. $3 per adult, 16 and younger free. National Parks Pass, Golden Eagle Passports, Golden Age and Golden Access Passports are honored. National Park Service, 928-634-5564. www.nps.gov/tuzi/home.htm.

Directions: Follow Hwy 89A west for 20 miles through Cottonwood toward Clarkdale, following signs for "Tuzigoot National Monument."

V-BAR-V RANCH View the astounding creativity of the ancients at a place where they pecked hundreds of beautiful rock art images into stone. Hours are currently 9:30am to 4:00pm (entrance gate closes at 3:30pm) on Friday, Saturday, Sunday and Monday. Closed Thanksgiving and Christmas. Guided tours are provided by the Verde Valley Archaeological Society and Friends of the Forest during these hours. The petroglyph area is fenced and only accessible during regular visiting hours. Entrance with Red Rock Pass. U.S. Forest Service, Sedona/Beaver Creek Ranger District, 928-282-4419. www.redrockcountry.org

Directions: Follow Hwy 179 south under the I-17 overpass. Hwy 179 becomes FR 618, which you should follow for 2.8 miles. Watch for the entrance on your right less than one-half mile past the Beaver Creek Campground.

Ballooning

Sedona's hot air balloons take off in the morning, when the air is most still. This means pickup times vary to coincide with sunrise.

★ **Red Rock Balloons** They say they fly closer to the red rocks of Sedona than any other balloon company. Hotel pickup and drop-off. Champagne continental breakfast included. Permitted in the Coconino National Forest. Free DVD per reservation. 105 Canyon Diablo Road, 928-284-0040, 800-258-3754.

★ **Northern Light/Sedona Balloons** Sedona's original balloon company has been flying around here since 1974. Champagne picnic is included. 928-282-2274, 800-230-6222.

Bicycling

With construction begun on a new and improved Hwy 179, bicyclists will have more options to tour red rock country. However, it must be said that in the meantime, this north-south route into Sedona is skinny and dangerous. With so many drivers watching the red rocks instead of the road, bicycling creates traffic jams and havoc. See "Mountain Biking" for shops with rentals, gear and advice.

EVENT
The Sedona Century Bicycle Tour This ride winds through Sedona and the surrounding Verde Valley. You can choose between a Metric Century and a 40-mile distance. Registration fee includes: official T-shirt, full ride support, rest stops, lunch and massage. There are contests and prizes as well a Friday night mixer. Event proceeds benefit the Old Town Mission, a local nonprofit organization that provides emergency resources and healthcare services to families and individuals suffering financial hardship. First Saturday in May. Contact Absolute Bikes, 928-284-1242, 877-284-1242.

Birding

Perhaps without realizing it, you've entered a birdwatcher's paradise. First, Sedona has a tremendous variety of terrain within a small area, and that means lots of different birds gather here. Second, pleasant weather and beautiful scenery make it especially easy and enjoyable to watch the birds. If you'd like a little orientation and guidance, your best bets are two local Arizona state parks.

BIRDS TO SEE

Among the many wonderful birds to look for, here are a few to whet your appetite. **Turkey vultures** (they call them buzzards in Texas) soar overhead. Birds of prey include the **red-tailed hawk** and the small falcon known as the **American kestrel**. The **eagle** and **black-hawk** make Sedona their home, but you'll need some luck to see one. You may see a few **roadrunners,** but more often the roads host families of **Gambel's quail** running across the street. Whether or not you hear the sad call of the **mourning dove** in the trees, you'll almost certainly encounter the noisy **scrub jay** or its black-crested cousin, the **Stellar's jay**. In the same zones, look for the beautiful **western bluebird** and the **Bullock's oriole**. Those big black birds soaring above aren't crows. They're **common ravens**. During the day, with your eye on Sedona's beautiful wildflowers, you may notice the small **black-chinned** or **green-throated hummingbirds**. By contrast, it is the dark of night that the **great horned owl** prefers. Count yourself lucky if you see one. In areas along the creek, look for small **Kingfishers** perched on branches as you await the large and graceful **great blue heron**. They like to go fishing around sunset.

PLACES TO GO

Red Rock State Park This park offers morning outings twice a week. The park has both riparian and high desert sections, allowing for a nice variety of bird habitats. In addition, the walking paths are quite gentle here. Walks are typically on Wednesday and Saturday, at either 7am or 8am, depending on the season. Bring binoculars if you have them; a few may be available to borrow. $7 per vehicle entrance fee. Drive west from the "Y" on Hwy 89A for five miles to Lower Red Rock Loop Road. Continue a few miles to the park entrance on the right. 928-282-2202. azstateparks.com

Slide Rock State Park This park hosts a bird walk on Saturdays when they have enough personnel. Remember that the park is up Oak Creek Canyon, so allow time if you're coming from the west side or the Village of Oak Creek. Also on Oak Creek, this park is a thousand feet higher in elevation than Red Rock State Park, making for different species of birds. $8 entrance fee per vehicle. Go seven miles north on Hwy 89A from the "Y." 928-282-3034. azstateparks.com

Page Springs Hatchery This Arizona Game & Fish facility, located west of Sedona in the village of Page Springs, features viewing platforms. Call for times and directions. 928-634-4805.

Dead Horse Ranch State Park Every spring, this park in Cottonwood hosts the annual Verde Valley Birding & Nature Festival, but birding is great year round. Favorite trails for birders are Tavasci Marsh and the Verde River Greenway. 928-634-5283.

BIRDING EVENTS

Verde Valley Birding Festival Although Dead Horse Ranch State Park in Cottonwood is the primary venue, Red Rock State Park and Slide Rock State Park also participate. The festival is held on the final Thursday through Sunday of April and includes field trips, workshops and of course, bird counts. Over 171 species were seen in three days one year. Field trips during the festival weekend have included visiting the Grand Canyon to see condors, viewing birds from the Verde Canyon Railroad train, and "power birding" in Prescott. For information, call Barbie Hart at 928-282-2002 or the special line at Parks and Recreation for the City of Cottonwood, 928-634-8437. www.birdyverde.org

Fishing

Drawing from local hatcheries, Arizona Game & Fish stocks Oak Creek upstream of the Pine Flat Campground, located high in Oak Creek Canyon. There are up to seven species of fish, including **brown trout** (wild) and **rainbows** (stocked). You'll find open as well as catch-and-release areas here. Even if you don't catch a thing, the beauty of Oak Creek makes the visit worthwhile. Some supplies are available from small stores in the canyon, but you're probably better off stocking up in town first.

88

LICENSES, GEAR AND GUIDES

Licenses are available in the Village of Oak Creek at Ace Hardware (6085 Hwy 179) and Webers/IGA grocery store. On the west side, head to Bashas' shopping center (corner of W Hwy 89A and Coffee Pot Drive). For information about fishing regulations or to apply for a license online, contact Arizona Game & Fish, 602-942-3000, www.gf.state.az.us.

Canyon Market If you're already lodging in Oak Creek Canyon, this market has bait, flies and hooks. Look for Don Hoel's Cabins, 9440 N Hwy 89A, OCC. 928-282-3560.

Sedona Sports This store offers licenses, rods and tackle, along with lots of advice. It is a good contact for arranging guide services. Across from Tlaquepaque, 251 Hwy 179, BTY. 928-282-1317. www.sedonasports.com

Gon' Fishen with Jim McGinness Licensed and friendly, Jim can help you find the fish. For all levels. Rates begin at $100 for one person for a half-day. 928-282-0788.

Indian Gardens–Oak Creek Visitor Center You can get a license, a Red Rock Pass and even rent a fishing pole at this small visitor center near Indian Gardens deli in Oak Creek Canyon.

TROUT FARM

Rainbow Trout Farm "Everything you will need to hook 'em and cook 'em." The fish are raised in artesian springs, and the farm features grills and picnic tables in a green setting. No license required. Open daily. Four miles north of Uptown at 3500 N Hwy 89A, OCC. 928-282-5799.

Golf

18-HOLE COURSES IN SEDONA

★ **Sedona Golf Resort** The area's finest golf course is a challenge, rising uphill through the front nine toward stunning red rock views. The par-71 course is 6,646 yards long. Rates: Late August-December 1, daily $105, $69 after 2pm. December-January, $93 for 18 holes, $59 after 1pm. February through mid-May, $105, $69 after 2pm. Mid-May through late August. $93 daily, $59 after 1pm. Late August through early December, $105, $69 after 2pm. Junior rate when playing with an adult, $20. Rental clubs available, $35-65. Range balls, 35 cents. Add sales tax to all fees. Rates include green fee, cart and range balls. Range balls included with green fee or $6 when not playing. Reservations taken up to 60 days in advance, or more than 60 for a group. 35 Ridge Trail Drive, VOC. 928-284-9355, 877-733-9885. www.sedonagolfresort.com

Oakcreek Country Club Things have improved greatly at OCCC (although they're sticking to the old way of spelling things in this part of town). This Robert Trent Jones designed–course is a 145-acre par-72, with three lakes. They've improved concrete cart paths, just in time for nifty new red carts. The fairways are classic tree-lined doglegs with fairway bunkers strategically placed in the landing areas, and the greens are all slightly elevated and surrounded by large swirling greenside bunkers. Host to the Sedona Open Golf Championship, held each July. Rates: March-November: $99 per person, 9 holes for $50. Twilight fee is $69. December-February: $79 per person for 18, 9 holes for $45. Twilight fee is $59. (Twilight hours vary throughout the year.) 690 Bell Rock Boulevard, VOC. 928-284-1660, 888-703-9489. www.sedonaopen.com

Seven Canyons This private course boasts one of the world's most beautiful settings. To try it, however, you'll have to fork up a cool $175,000 to join. Housing around the course consists of private homes and fractional ownership villas. Curious? 3755 Long Canyon Road, WS. 928-203-2000. www.sevencanyons.com

18-HOLE COURSES NEARBY

Beaver Creek Country Club An improved 18-hole course, 35 minutes south. 18-hole rates, including a cart are: Mon-Thurs $39; Fri-Sun $49, Rental clubs are $25. Twilight rates begin after 1pm:

89

Mon-Thurs $25; Fri-Sun $35. 4105 E. Lakeshore Drive, Lake
Montezuma. 928-567-4487.

Verde Santa Fe Golf Course Subtract the red rocks and substitute
more reasonable playing rates. Rates: Mon-Thurs, 18 Holes $50
with cart, Fri-Sun $60. Twilight begins early here, after 12 noon,
when the rate drops to $45. 1045 S. Verde Santa Fe Parkway,
Cornville, AZ. 12.5 miles west of I-17 at McGuireville Exit.
928-634-5454. www.verdesantafe.com

90

EXECUTIVE COURSES
Canyon Mesa Short and fun in a private community. 9 holes,
1475 yards total. $15 for 9 holes, $20 for 18 holes. Rentals $10.
500 Jacks Canyon Road, VOC. 928-284-0036.

The Radisson Poco Diablo A short, crisscrossing executive course.
9 holes, 777 yards. Play as many holes as you like for $20, or $10
per round after 2pm. $5 rentals. 1736 Hwy 179, BTY. 928-282-7333.

MINIATURE GOLF
Premiere Country Club No kidding, they have a genuine
championship here in the summer with actual prize money. There's
a bocce court here too. Los Abrdigados, 160 Portal Lane, BTY.
282-5108, ext 6.

Got Water?

With Sedona's elevation and dry climate, dehydration can
creep up on unwary visitors. The Sedona Westerners, a local
hiking group, suggests carrying at least a quart of water on
short hikes, more for longer hikes or during hot weather.
The first signs of dehydration are as subtle as becoming a
wee bit cranky. Have mercy on your hiking companions and
carry plenty of water!

Hiking

If you do nothing else in Sedona, get out of the car and go for a walk. There are nearly a hundred trails just waiting to be hiked. If you'd like to make the most of a trail, I strongly recommend my popular hiking guide, *Sedona's Top 10 Hikes*. It is full of gorgeous photos, in-depth descriptions to keep you from getting lost, and lots of interesting history, vortex information and geological descriptions.

91

Sedona's altitude (approximately 4,500 feet above sea level) keeps the air clean but will work your lungs a bit more. It also accelerates dehydration, so always bring plenty of water and sip often. Finally, make certain you sign in and tell your innkeeper/hosts which trail you intend to take.

GENTLE TRAILS

Mother Nature doesn't really make "flat" here, but you can turn around at any time on any of these trails, and none have substantial hills.

Highlight

Around here, the moon can be so bright that the trails are easy to follow. Join Red Rock State Park for their full moon hikes, offered monthly in the days leading up to and including the big night. 928-282-2202.

Fay Canyon Trail (WS) This trail is gentle and offers a wilderness setting in lovely Fay Canyon. A highlight is the afternoon glow on the the eastern wall. There's no clear end to the trail. Turn around when it seems too tricky to follow, and you'll wind up with a two-mile round trip. Head west for about a half-mile on the dirt road near Enchantment Resort. Trail parking on right. No toilets here.

Bell Rock Pathway (VOC) If you're a novice and wary of being alone in the wilderness, start here. The crowds will be here, but there's lots of room on a wide pathway. Walk to Bell Rock and back for a two-mile walk, or do a moderate hike by going all the way around Courthouse Butte (four miles). Large parking lot, just north of Circle K on Hwy 179, VOC. No toilets here.

West Fork (OCC) Gorgeous and romantic, this historic trail follows a gentle stream. Crowded on weekends and in autumn for its foliage. Six miles roundtrip. There is little elevation gain, but there is lots of

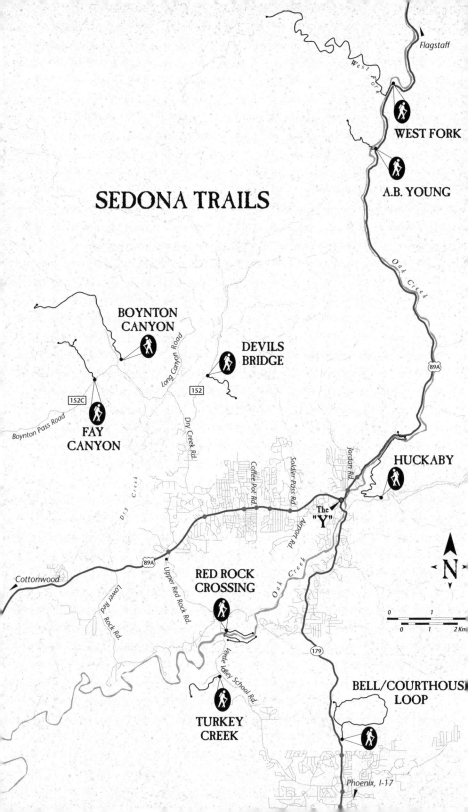

stepping on stones to cross the creek back and forth. Drive north on Hwy 89A for 10 miles to the Call of the Canyon entry lot on the left. There are toilets here.

MODERATE TRAILS

These trails are at least three miles round trip, with 200 to 500 feet of elevation change.

Vultee Arch (WS) Hike through the forest with a natural arch in the distance as your final reward. About three miles round trip. The drive out, however, is long, five miles on the dirt. Follow 89A to Dry Creek Road. Turn right onto the signed dirt road. No toilets here.

Soldiers Pass (WS) Home of the interesting Seven Sacred Pools and the Devil's Kitchen natural sinkhole. Start to the right by the trail kiosk and come home via the wider jeep road trail. Less than a half-mile in, look left to find Devil's Kitchen. (Many people accidentally turn right and unknowingly wind up on the Jordan Trail). This is a three-mile loop if you turn back at the yellow fence, or five miles if you follow the trail through the fence up the canyon. Head up Soldier Pass Road, 1.2 miles west of the "Y." Go 1.4 miles to Rim Shadows Drive, then right 0.2 miles (continue forward although the street branches left). On the left is the entry to this gated parking lot. No toilets here.

Long Canyon Trail (WS) The farther in you go, the better it gets in this towering canyon. As with Fay Canyon, Long Canyon has no clear end point. Turn around when it starts feeling more like a struggle than a hike. Over five miles roundtrip, 500 feet of elevation gain. Go west on Hwy 89A and turn right onto Dry Creek Road, then right onto Long Canyon Road at stop sign. Continue about a half-mile to dirt parking lot on left. No toilets here.

Boynton Canyon (WS) This beautiful canyon is famous but sometimes overcrowded. Since the first mile merely walks the border of Enchantment Resort, don't hike Boynton unless you're sure you can go further in. Beware the early setting sun

Big Mistake

Each year, many tourists head to Boynton Canyon to watch the sunset. Take note that this beautiful canyon actually completely blocks the sunset. Misguided guide book writers should have said, however, that the east walls are rich in color in late afternoon, often as long as two hours before the actual sunset.

and cooler temps. It's five to six miles round trip, and most of the 400-plus feet of elevation gain comes in the last 15 minutes on the way in. In West Sedona, take Dry Creek Road north, following signs for Enchantment Resort. After the second stop sign, you'll see the parking lot on the right. There are toilets at the parking lot.

Turkey Creek (VOC) Need a quiet trail near the Village? Turkey Creek is lovely and free of tourists. You can hike up to six miles round trip, with the option for a moderate uphill in the final half-mile going in. Follow Verde Valley School Road. Less than a mile after it turns to dirt (but still passable), take the left-hand turn at the Turkey Creek Trail sign. No toilets here.

HILLY TRAILS

From short to long, these trails are partially or entirely steep.

Devil's Bridge (WS) This is the best choice in inclement weather, or for those with vertigo or unsure footing. Don't quit till you get to the natural stone bridge, which is awesome to behold. The trail is under two miles round trip, 350 feet up. Drive west on 89A, turning right at Dry Creek Road on the far west side of Sedona. Take a right onto the dirt road FR 152. You'll find limited trail parking on the right, three rough miles ahead. No toilets here.

Huckaby (BTY) This groovy trail has plenty of up and down to it. Each turn seems to reveal a new view. Walk down to the creek and return, or cross the creek to climb high up to Midgely Bridge. Walk four to five miles, depending on your turn-around point. Drive from the "Y" and turn left onto Schnebly Hill Road, just over the bridge. Follow to the parking lot at the end of the paved road. Toilets are at the parking lot.

A.B. Young (OCC) This big slog of a hike brings you up 1,600 feet to stand above the entire Oak Creek Canyon. To begin, go behind Bootlegger Campground and hop across the creek. Step up to the wide path running on the other side, and look for the rusty trailhead sign. At the top, you can go west for nearly a mile to a fire lookout tower. It is four to five miles round trip. Drive up 89A to Oak Creek Canyon to milepost 383.3 to Bootlegger Campground. Toilets are at the campground.

HIKING GUIDES

Here are the town's top three hiking guides. For further recommendations, check at the Sedona Outfitter Guide Association, at www.soga.com

★ **Mr. Sedona** This is my company, and I offer a private experience for individuals, couples or families, focusing on seeing the places most people never get to see. Along the way, I offer a wealth of information on geology, plant life, wildlife, Native American history and vortexes. As a private service, we travel at exactly the pace you prefer, and focus on what you'll most enjoy in nature. Prices begin at $275 for a couple. 928-204-2201. www.MrSedona.com

Southwest Outside Mike Krajnak is friendly, diligent and experienced. 928-284-1816. www.southwestoutside.com

Touch the Earth Steve "Benny" Benedict works most often with guests at stylish El Portal, but he may have availability. He is highly experienced and friendly. 928-203-9312. www.earthtours.com

95

Highlight

Sedona may be America's best place to go for a day hike. Great weather, trails for all levels and gorgeous views are just a few of the reasons. While all kinds of vehicles can take you over the rocks, it is still hard to beat the good feelings that come with putting your soles on them yourself. Even if you don't consider yourself a "hiker," Sedona is the place to try a trail.

GEAR

Do yourself a BIG favor: Bring good walking shoes, not flat tennies. Find them at these spots.

Canyon Outfitters 2701 W Hwy 89A, WS. 928-282-5293..

★ **Sedona Sports** Their staff are experts in feet. Across from Tlaquepaque, 251 Hwy 179, BTY. 928-282-1317. www.sedonasports.com

Horseback Rides

★ **Equinature, USA** At last, the horse whisperers have arrived. Equinature is an intriguing operation with very good personal service. They'll pick you up and take you to Sycamore Canyon for a private or semi-private ride. Though it costs more, this is the superior kind of experience Sedona has been waiting for. All riding levels are welcome. Half-day and full-day rides start at $200. 12250 Serenity Lane, Cornville. 928-639-9517. www.equinature-france-arizona.com

M Diamond Ranch This genuine working ranch is located in Beaver Creek, a 30-minute van ride (they'll pick you up) south from Sedona. Rates for trail rides are $64 for one hour, $85 for two hours. 928-300-6466. www.mdiamondranch.com

Institutes and Museums

Institute of Eco-Tourism This center provides education and outreach to support sustainable tourism. Exhibits, theater, books and gifts are offered, along with weekly speakers. Admission free. Daily, 10am-6pm. Next door to Los Abrigados, 95 Portal Lane, BTY. 928-282-2720. www.ioet.org

Ringing Rocks Foundation This small but interesting center celebrates the practices of native and shamanic healers from a stunning variety of cultures around the world. Admission free. Mon-Sat 10am-5pm. 1890 W Hwy 89A, WS. 928-282-1298. www.ringingrocks.org

Sedona Heritage Museum Exhibits on settler life, fun items from the many Westerns filmed here, and more. History buffs should not miss jeep-guide, storyteller and performer Michael Peach recreate historical characters and their tales. Open daily, 11am-3pm. Admission: $3. 735 Jordan Road, UP. 928-282-7038. www.sedonamuseum.org

Jeeps and Off-Roading

IN YOUR OWN VEHICLE

If you're arriving in a 4WD vehicle, you have plenty of options. Most of all, I'd recommend heading beyond the west side of town. Take Dry Creek Road (three miles west on 89A) to find dirt roads in the Red Rock–Secret Mountain Wilderness. Please stay on the main (dirt) road. Going off-road does huge amounts of damage to fragile terrain and destroys plant life. A good investment is a map: Beartooth offers a good one, sold at outdoor stores, and the pertinent Forest Service topographical maps can help too.

Highlight

Welcome to the land of Roadrunner and Coyote. Keep your eyes open at the start and finish of the day. You may see roadrunners in early mornings and late evenings in the Village of Oak Creek, and coyotes around West Sedona.

JEEP RENTALS

Farabee Jeep Rentals of Sedona Rent a Jeep for your own self-guided tour. Half-day rates starting at $99, including free maps, trail info, and ice chest with ice. 3009 W Hwy 89A, UP. 928-282-8700, 800-806-JEEP.

A Day in the West Offering jeep rentals at comparable rates, based in Uptown. 252 N Hwy 89A, UP. 928-282-4320, 800-973-3662.

JEEP TOURS

Sedona's most famous tourist activity now comes in a variety of colors, including red, yellow and pink. Truth is, if you've only got a couple of hours in town and don't know where to go, a jeep tour is a fun option. They are not ideal for those who don't like bumps.

A Day in the West This company offers rides, cookouts, and special events. Most tours are $40-75, with discounts for kids. 252 N Hwy 89A, UP. 928-282-4320, 800-973-3662.

★ **Pink Jeep Tours** Try the Broken Arrow Tour for a scenic and hilly adventure. $72 plus tax, $54 plus tax for kids. 204 N Hwy 89A, UP. 928-282-5000, 800-873-3662.

Sedona Red Rock Jeep Tours The cowboy flavor is appealing at Red Rock Jeeps. They feature the Soldiers Pass area outing which includes a sinkhole, Seven Sacred Pools and views into a lovely canyon. $58 plus tax, $43 plus tax for kids. 270 N Hwy 89A, UP. 928-282-6826, 800-848-7728.

HUMMER and ATV TOURS

Hummer Affair 273 N Hwy 89A, Suite C, UP. 928-282-6656, 928-204-2555.
Arizona ATV Adventures 1185 W Hwy 89A, WS. 800-242-6335.

Motorcycling

GOOD RIDES

Oak Creek Canyon A ride through Oak Creek Canyon lifts you 15 miles up switchbacks onto the Colorado Plateau, and 13 miles after that you're in old Route 66 country in Flagstaff.

Jerome A very popular ride is west to Jerome, where bikers are very welcome. Head west on 89A and follow signs through Cottonwood. "The Spirit Room" bar is often the center of activity. Note that Jerome enforces a noise ordinance.

RENTALS and REPAIRS

EagleRider This moto-outfitter specializes in renting Harley-Davidsons. With locations in tourist spots in the USA, you can try one-way rentals between franchise rental facilities. The company also offers guided motorcycle tours through Arizona, Nevada and California. 6560 Hwy 179, VOC. 928-284-3983, 888-900-9901.

APPAREL

Grand Canyon Harley-Davidson Live the life, wear the clothes. 320 N Hwy 89A, UP. 928-204-0020.

Mountain Biking

THE SCOOP

No longer can "experienced" mountain bikers avoid a pilgrimage to Sedona to taste one of America's best spots for a ride. The word is out.

SHOPS & RENTAL INFO

Mountain Bike Heaven Sedona's oldest bike shop appeals to the hard-core crowd. These are the Kings of MTB culture with very good service and their own line of videos, T-shirts and coffee mugs. Group rides depart from here mid-week and on weekends. Note that these are challenging: Unfit riders won't even make it to the trailhead. Normal dual suspension rentals are $7.50 an hour, or $25 for a 24-hour day, and upscale duallies are $10/$35. Your rental includes a helmet, spare tube, pump, patch kit and trail map. Open daily at 8am, closing time varies between 5 and 6pm, depending on the season. Closes on Sundays at 4pm. 1695 W. Hwy 89A, WS. 928-282-1312. www.mountainbikeheaven.com

Sedona Bike and Bean This shop has distinguished itself with good service from well-informed employees. It is also the best choice if you want to start out easy—you can rent a bike and just cross the street to try out the Bell Rock Pathway. They feature a scale model of Sedona and its trails, allowing you to feel as if you were viewing Red Rock Country from above. Bike and Bean offers gear and their own fresh roasted coffee plus espresso, cappuccino, latte, mocha and americano made from their Bike and Bean Blend. Full suspension bikes are $50 per day, $40 for four hours or less. (Group and multi-day rates available—call for details.) Front suspension bikes are $40 per day, $30 for four hours or less, $25 for two hours. Open 9am-5pm (Nov-1-Feb 28), 8am-6pm (Mar 1-Oct 31). 6020 Hwy 179, VOC. 928-284-0210. www.bike-bean.com

Absolute Bikes Sponsors of the Sedona Century hundred-mile ride. Reservations require a credit card. You'll need a matching picture ID and credit card to use as a deposit on the equipment you rent. Meet at the shop for Sunday morning off-road rides and Monday morning road rides. Contact Susan Amon at amonlsusan@aol.com or call 928-284-4085 for all the details. 6101 Hwy 179, VOC. 928-284-1242, 877-284-1242.

Sedona Sports This shop offers a good deal for a bike rental package, and facilitates tours. Across from Tlaquepaque, 251 Hwy 179, BTY. 928-282-1317. www.sedonasports.com

MOUNTAIN BIKING TOURS

Sedona MTB Adventures Over 200 miles of trails await with these expert guides, who cater to all levels, from beginner to advanced. Families are welcome. Half-day tour: First rider $75, $35 each additional rider. Full-day tour: One rider: $150, $50 each additional rider. Broken Arrow Loop Tour: One rider: $100, $40 each additional rider. Intro to Mountain Biking: One rider: $75, $35 each additional rider. Prices do not include the bike, which can be rented. Discounts for groups. 50 Skyline Circle, VOC. 928-284-1246.

100

Native American Tours

Native Visions This tour outfitter is based at the nearby Yavapai-Apache Nation. They offer van tours and horseback rides, as well as exposure to Native arts and crafts. 928-567-3035. www.nativevisionstours.com

Way of the Ancients This company offers escorted touring van trips to get you to all those great Arizona places beyond Sedona. They offer a tour to nearby Montezuma Well and Montezuma Castle ruins. Beyond the Verde Valley, they offer tours to the Grand Canyon, Monument Valley, Canyon de Chelly (dee-SHAY), the Painted Desert and the Colorado River. 928-204-9243, 866-204-9243. www.wayoftheancients.com

Key to Symbols

★ = Highly Recommended

((($))) = Great Value

Parks and Passes

Discovering Sedona's wilderness can be surprisingly complicated. The chief reason for the complexity is that Sedona's public lands are maintained by several different agencies. Most of the hiking you'll be doing involves the Coconino National Forest. To park on it, you'll need a Red Rock Pass. Also run by the Forest Service, and covered by the pass, are the wonderful ruins at Palatki. Some of the most famous nature spots are operated by private contractors to the Forest Service, and they charge a separate entry fee. This includes places like West Fork and Crescent Moon Ranch. Add to this a pair of Arizona State Parks, Slide Rock and Red Rock State Park. The pass isn't valid at either of these. More on most of these locations can be found at www.redrockcountry.org.

If you're confused about which pass works where, you're not alone. If still stuck by the time you're ready to leave for an adventure, follow this simple recommendation: Make sure you've got a ten dollar bill in your wallet when you head out, and you'll be fine.

THE LOCATIONS

Coconino National Forest Home to nearly a hundred great hiking trails, the forest accounts for most of the untouched greenery left in and around Sedona. Munds Mountain Wilderness and Red Rock–Secret Mountain Wilderness areas are the predominant portions of the national forest in our area, covering more than 68,000 acres. 928-282-4119. www.redrockcountry.org

Crescent Moon Ranch/Red Rock Crossing/Cathedral Rock A short tutorial: The signature red rock formation which you see on so many postcards is Cathedral Rock. The place we love to photograph it from is Red Rock Crossing, where Oak Creek flows below Cathedral Rock. The place to go to see Red Rock Crossing is Crescent Moon Ranch. Here you'll find a park, parking, picnic areas and environmental toilets. As with West Fork, a contractor manages the park and charges a $7 fee for cars. It's $1 if you cross the creek or otherwise walk in. Drive west on Hwy 89A for four miles and turn left at Upper Red Rock Loop Road. Turn left onto Chavez Ranch Road and follow it to just short of the dead end, staying on the pavement. WS

Grasshopper Point This recreation site features a swimming hole, and perhaps that's why it isn't open year round. Here you'll find a very fun (or very scary) jump from the cliffs into the creek. It also provides some nice foliage in the autumn. Allen's Bend Trail begins here. Drive two miles north from Uptown on Hwy 89A. Fee is $5 or $7 (depending on season) per vehicle, or included with Grand Annual Pass. OCC

Red Rock State Park Arizona's famous Oak Creek meanders through Red Rock State Park, creating a diverse riparian habitat for plants and wildlife. Located on the west side of town, this park has a nice resource center with good information about local plant and animal life. Rangers and volunteers lead daily instructional walks on the park's very gentle paths (usually at 10am and 2pm). Wednesdays and Saturdays at 8 am, you can join a guided bird walk. Park hours are 8 am to 5pm; Visitor Center hours are 9am to 5pm. For details on programs, call the Interpretive Education Office (928-282-2202). Drive west on Hwy 89A for five miles, turning left onto Lower Red Rock Loop Road. Follow it to the park entrance on the right. Fee is $7 per car. Closed Christmas Day. WS. 928-282-6907.

Slide Rock For more than a half a century, Arizonans have chosen this spot as the place to beat the heat. Located in Oak Creek Canyon, here the creek has carved a chute through the red sandstone that's ideal for slipping and sliding in the wet stuff. There's lots of history around here, where some of Sedona's first settlers lived. You'll find some of the first apple orchards they planted, the fruits of which are sold at the Slide Rock Market within the park. The water quality hotline is 602-542-0202 if you'd like to check before you arrive from Phoenix. Summer: 8am-7pm. Autumn and Spring: 8am-6pm. Winter: 8am-5pm, with last entry at 4pm. Fee is $8 per vehicle; Slide Rock Market opens at 10am each day. Drive seven miles north on Hwy 89A, OCC. Recorded message at 928-282-3034. azstateparks.com

West Fork/Call of the Canyon Made famous by author Zane Grey, this area features a gentle stream winding through a lovely canyon. It is one of the state's most historic and beautiful trails. Within the Coconino National Forest, this day-use area is administered by a private concessionaire and costs $7 per vehicle to enter. North on Hwy 89A, OCC, 11 miles from Uptown.

Picnicking is also possible at a few other day use areas: Banjo Bill ($5 per car), Encinoso (Red Rock Pass required) and Halfway Picnic Area (Red Rock Pass required). All are in Oak Creek Canyon along N. Hwy 89A.

There are no national parks or monuments in Sedona, but plenty within driving distance. East is Tuzigoot and south are Montezuma Castle and Montezuma Well. See "Ancient Ruins" for more. Between here and the Grand Canyon are Walnut Canyon, Wupatki and Sunset Crater.

THE RED ROCK PASS

The Forest Service's website suggests that "a pass is not required for incidental stopping to take a photograph or to enjoy a scenic vista (approximately 15 minutes or less)." A one-day pass costs $5 (for one calendar day); a weekly pass costs $15; the annual pass costs $20. The grand annual pass costs $40, and is best for local and long-term visitors who want a 12-month pass and unlimited entry into Red Rock Country Heritage Sites (V–V, Palatki and Honanki) and day-use sites operated by the concessionaires. It is not valid for the use of other fee areas or developed campgrounds. The pass should be hung on your car's rear-view mirror. The pass covers all trailhead parking and even car pullouts in the Coconino National Forest, Palatki, Honanki, and V–V ("V Bar V"). Daily and weekly passes can be purchased from self-serve machines at some trailheads, and passes are sold at many accommodations, retail, convenience and sporting goods stores in the area.

The list of what the standard Red Rock Pass doesn't cover includes campgrounds and day use areas such as Banjo Bill, West Fork/Call of the Canyon, Crescent Moon Ranch/Red Rock Crossing and Grasshopper Point. These cost between $5 and $8 per vehicle. Red Rock State Park and Slide Rock are Arizona state parks not covered by the pass: they cost $7 and $8 per vehicle, respectively.

Most of Sedona's wild area is national forest, not national park. But your Golden Age or Golden Eagle passports will be accepted at many sites in Sedona, although these are generally sold by the National Park Service. Got it?

Rock Climbing

Sedona's red rocks are composed of soft sandstone that fractures easily, making climbing treacherous. Nonetheless, there are those people who can do it in those special places where it is doable. Route lengths range from 1 to over 10 pitches, and cracks are wide. The most famous multi-pitch climb is The Mace, a spire of Cathedral Rock. Better options appear heading north into Oak Creek Canyon. Nearby Flagstaff is small, but its climbing community is big if you're looking for a partner.

104

GEAR
Canyon Outfitters The author of *Red Lizard's Climbing Guide* works here. 2701 W Hwy 89A, WS. 928-282-5293.
Sedona Sports The store located across from Tlaquepaque offers guidebooks and gear. 251 Hwy 179, BTY. 928-282-1317. www.sedonasports.com

GUIDES
Terra Trax Offers private and team climbing adventures, including "Learn the Ropes." The half-day experience costs between $80 and $150 per person. 928-284-5606.

Running

ROUTES
Trail-running is what people find most fun around here. Give it a try and you may have a hard time going back to just going up and down the block back home. Check "Hiking" for trail suggestions. If you still feel the need for circles, however, check out the adequate high school track. Head west on 89A, turning left at the intersection of Upper Red Rock Loop Road. Track is to the west of the parking lot.

For a two-mile, somewhat hilly loop that combines paved and dirt surfaces, try the Morris Morning Special. Drive south from the "Y" along 179 to turn left at Sombart Lane, the street beyond the Circle

K. Park in the lot, and head through the gate onto the Marg's Draw trail. The trail heads uphill just 75 feet. At the major "T" about a quarter-mile along, turn left. You'll follow along under Snoopy Rock until you come to the paved Schnebly Hill Road. Turn left and follow the pavement downhill to the intersection with Hwy 179. Turn left and continue to the Circle K, turning left again to return to the parking lot.

EVENTS

The inaugural Sedona Marathon was held in February 2006 and was a big success. It is a qualifier for Boston. The challenging 2006 course was an out-and-back set-up leading from the western entry to town into beautiful red rock hill country, with more than half the course on gravel and dirt. Half-marathon and 5K routes are available as well. 2675 W Hwy 89A, Suite #451, WS. 928-203-9993, 800-775-7671. www.SedonaMarathon.com

GEAR

Cabana Shoes & Activewear Basha's Plaza, 162 Coffee Pot Drive, WS. 928-282-6956
Sedona Sports Trail running shoes are best found here. Across from Tlaquepaque, 251 Hwy 179, BTY. 928-282-1317. www.sedonasports.com

Skydiving and Powerchuting

Adrenaline junkies, we've heard your prayers.

Powerchute Sedona What's the buzz I've been hearing in the morning? No, not a bee, but a powered parachute! A what? Join a pilot as the passenger on a trip with splendid views. Rates: $89-$159. Follow 89A south of town toward Cottonwood. Take a right on FR 525 and proceed for 2.7 miles. Turn left on FR 525C. Take a left onto FR 525A. The airfield will be on the right. 928-300-8119.
Skydive Sedona What it would be like to see the red rocks in free fall? Find out with this outfitter at Cottonwood Airport. If you are new to skydiving, a tandem outing (with you on the back of an

experienced instructor) will be your best bet, with rates beginning at $199. Although there is a minimum load requirement, experienced sky-divers will find that they are open daily, year-round. From Sedona, take Hwy 89A south. At the first stoplight, turn right on Mingus Ave. Go about three to four miles. You will go through the intersection at Main St. and the intersection of 89A again. After that intersection, go about 0.25 mile. You will see the gate for the main airport building on your left. Look for the next gate just past the main entrance. 1001 W Mingus Ave., Cottonwood. 928-649-8899.

Stargazing

Sedona has a dark-sky ordinance that aims to keep our lights dim enough to maintain the views of wonderful starry skies. If you're on your own, I can suggest two good places to watch the stars. The first is at the overlook on Airport Mesa (see "Sightseeing" for directions). Here you'll see the lights of Sedona shimmering below, as well as the stars above. Second, pull off along the side of Dry Creek Road (three miles west of the "Y"). Here, away from any town light, you'll notice what appears to be a constellation low on the western horizon. Actually, it's the old mining town of Jerome on the hillside. Nearby Flagstaff hosts Lowell Observatory, where the planet Pluto was discovered in 1930. 928-774-3358, www.lowell.edu.

Evening Sky Tours These guides to the night sky offer you the chance to see not just stars, but planets. They will bring their telescopes to your hotel, or you can meet them at their out-of-town spot. This 90-minute show costs $45-60 per adult and $20 per child. Their astronomers will answer all your questions. Your money is returned if it is too cloudy to see. 928-853-9778, 866-701-0398.

Tennis

Sedona has two sets of public courts. The first are on Posse Grounds Drive. Turn north off Hwy 89A and follow Posse Grounds till it ends. Courts are between the school and the athletic field. For the second, take Hwy 89A to Sunset Drive, turn left and drive one mile toward Airport Mesa. Look for the new park on your right. Visitors can pay to play at Los Abrigados, Poco Diablo and Sedona Racquet Club. Enchantment Resort occasionally hosts tournaments and round robins open to visitors not staying at the resort. It would also be the place to stay if you're hoping for lessons. Call the pro shop at 928-204-6015 for more information.

Trains

Verde Canyon Railroad The train travels a historic route from Clarkdale to Perkinsville and back, featuring native flora and fauna, ancient Indian ruins, red rock pinnacles and a 680-foot manmade tunnel. You can choose from first-class or coach service. Either way, insiders know to check ahead. Clay Miller's narration and story-telling make the trip. 300 N Broadway, Clarkdale. 928-639-0010, 800-293-7245. www.verdecanyonrr.com

Trolley ands Van Tours

《$》 **The Sedona Trolley** The trolley's slogan is "The Best First Thing To Do In Sedona." Apparently, there are now two first things to consider, i.e., two 55-minute tours from which to pick. The southside tour includes the Chapel of the Holy Cross and Tlaquepaque, while the second tour heads out to the scenic canyons around Enchantment Resort. Located Uptown at the traffic light near Canyon Breeze restaurant. 928-282-4211, 928-282-5400.

(($)) **Redstone Tours** These guided van tours cover Sedona and Grand Canyon. The Sedona tour ($24 plus tax) lasts two hours and includes the Chapel of the Holy Cross, Airport Vortex, Oak Creek Canyon, Tlaquepaque, Bell Rock and other locations. A deluxe tour is $84 plus tax for seven hours, including gourmet picnic lunch. 928-203-0396, 866-473-3786.

Vortexes

UNDERSTANDING THE CONCEPT

Sedona's most fascinating, controversial, delightful and confusing subject is its vortexes (or if you prefer, vortices). For years, visitors have experienced strong feelings here that seem to be inspired by the beauty of the rocks, and yet not fully explained by it. From an increase in intuition to a sense of being at home, thousands report the phenomenon.

Geological study has demonstrated—in contrast to what you may hear from locals—that magnetism is not the source of the phenomenon. Likewise, to call certain spots magnetic or electric electromagnetic (or masculine and feminine) is inaccurate. Yet it is equally clear that people aren't just "making this up." Documented reactions suggest that those who are more sensitive to energy feel something here that makes Sedona more than such a pretty place. What are the reactions? They range from people moved spontaneously to emotion to feeling unusually healthy and vibrant to having surprisingly potent intuitions.

A bit of advice. Consider a private tour, but recognize that there are as many "experts" as there are citizens. If you choose to simply visit vortex spots and wait for it to "hit you," you'll see pretty places, but you may be disappointed. There is no correct spot to stand on and no correct way to feel it.

PRIVATE VORTEX TOURS

For all tours, we most recommend members of the Sedona Metaphysical Spiritual Association.

★ **Mr. Sedona** Dennis Andres (author) offers an in-depth experience that focuses on issues you'd like to heal or release and new dreams you'd like to create. It is one part tour (as you'll visit scenic spots around the area), one part nature walk (from very, very gentle to strenuous, as you prefer), and one part personal growth experience (with conversation, deep listening and guided visualization included). Your guide is the author of Sedona's best-seller, *What Is A Vortex? A Practical Guide to Sedona's Energy Sites,* and also the author of the book in your hands. You'll travel comfortably in a Jeep Grand Cherokee and be picked up at your accommodation. Half-day private outings begin at $275 for two. A fun experience.

109

Pete Sanders, Jr. Pete is the author of *Scientific Vortex Information* and a founding member of the Sedona Metaphysical Spiritual Association. For prices and information, contact Pete directly at 928-282-9425.

Sedona Sacred Journeys Gregory Drambour recovered from cancer, and his specialty is offering outings particularly tailored for those with severe health issues who are looking for an alternative, energetic cure. Prices are high, but so are the results offered. Center for the New Age, BTY. www.sedona-spiritual-vacations.com

VAN and JEEP VORTEX TOURS

Earth Wisdom Tours This jeep company offers a more spiritual approach. 293 N Hwy 89A, UP. 928-282-4714.

Vortex Tours/Sedona Retreats This west-side company offers daily van tours lasting about three hours. 1385 W Hwy 89A, WS. 928-282-2733, 800-943-3266.

Walking

If a hike seems too strenuous, here are some gentle pathways for you.
Crescent Moon Ranch (WS) Here concrete sidewalks and dirt
paths stretch alongside Oak Creek in view of majestic Cathedral
Rock. Drive west on Hwy 89A to Upper Red Rock Loop Road.
Turn left, then left again onto Chavez Ranch Road, and follow it
around the curve to the entry station. Fee is required to park.

Carruth Trail (WS) This gentle path has fine views, and the plants
are labeled. More trails like this will put a guide like me out of
business! Drive west on Hwy 89A from the "Y," for 1.2 miles,
turning right onto Posse Grounds Road. Just before the elementary
school, turn right and look for the trail entrance on the left-hand
side. Pull over here to park.

The Labryinth, Lodge at Sedona (WS) Like walking in circles?
There's a labyrinth here if you'd like to truly prove that "not all who
wander all lost." Please be considerate, as the Lodge is a private
property. Call ahead if you'd like to bring a group. Drive west on
Hwy 89A, turn left on Kallof Place and proceed through the parking
lot. The labyrinth is in the back of the property.

Red Rock State Park (WS) Here you'll find gentle walking in
both desert and riparian terrain. Birding walks are are typically on
Wednesday and Saturday, at either 7am or 8am, depending on the
season. $7 per vehicle entrance fee. From the "Y," drive west on
Hwy 89A for five miles to Lower Red Rock Loop Road. Continue a
few miles to the park entrance, which is on the right. 928-282-2202.
azstateparks.com

Wild Animals

Sedona's three-part terrain of high desert, riparian and mountainous
zones leads to a remarkable diversity of wildlife. With a little extra
effort, you may be able to see some of it. For a primer on local animals,
see the "Questions & Answers" section.

Wildlife Park

Out of Africa Wildlife Park This park creates 40 acres of habitat for giraffe, wildebeest, zebra and other animals of the African plains. Join an educational tram and trolley tour or take a walk and photograph the predators from unobstructed photo platforms. See exotic animals as you ride in a safari vehicle driven by guides. Admission: Adults $28, kids (3-12) $20, seniors $26. Hours: Wed-Sun 9:30am-5pm (closed Mon-Tues). Open all year, except for Thanksgiving, Christmas, and July 4th. Located three miles west of I-17 on Hwy 260 in Camp Verde. Leave the interstate at exit 287 and turn right, toward Cottonwood. Turn left on Verde Valley Justice Center Road, then immediately right into the park.

Wineries and Vineyards

Oak Creek Vineyards & Winery Six wine grape varieties—Chardonnay, Fumé Blanc, White Zinfandel, Merlot, Syrah and Zinfandel—bask proudly on terraced slopes directly across from Oak Creek. The winery, established in 2002, also carries a great assortment of wine essentials from decanters to openers. Wed-Sun, 11am-5pm. Across from the Page Spring Fish Hatchery on Page Springs Road, Cornville, Off of Rt. 89A. 928-649-0290.

Page Springs Winery Eric Glomski has an intense relationship with the wines of the Rhone region. While he's faithful to his love, he's not jealous. He's happy to share. They work with Syrah, Petite Sirah, Grenache, Mourvedre and other reds such as Cabernet Pfeffer, Counoise and Cinsault. White grapes include Viognier, Rousanne and Marsanne. Excellent wine tasting daily, 11am-6pm. 1500 N Page Springs Road, Cornville. 928-639-3004.

5

Treasures of Sedona's Colony of Culture

Art

The growth and development in Sedona may have obscured but can never undo that the arts community is what makes this more than just another pretty town. With a stunning array of diversity for such a small population, Sedona's artists are expressing, creating and succeeding. Here we list key events, excit-

ing galleries and special artists to watch for that will be your passport into the Sedona art colony. Do your browsing and shopping early because most shops and galleries close early. In other words, shop first, then dine.

Highlight

In 2006 the Sedona Gallery Association moved its open evening event to the first Friday of each month. The Art Walk typically involves a dozen or more participants, and some galleries use the date to open new exhibitions.

Art Organizations

Sedona Arts Center In 1958 Egyptian-born sculptor Nassan Gobran and a group of visionaries, inspired by the natural beauty of Sedona, saw the need for a place where artists could work and teach together—an arts center. Today, SAC's Creativity Series workshops are designed to help students realize their creative dreams. Featuring nationally known facilitators, such as Julia Cameron and Natalie Goldberg, classes offer inspiration to students searching for their artistic voice. Field workshops combine artistic and cultural adventures from the Grand Canyon to Tuscany. Over 50 intensive fine art workshops are offered annually in a wide variety of styles and mediums.

The Sedona Arts Alliance Sometimes getting artists to unite is like herding cats. In Sedona, one organization unites all the arts organizations. sedonaartsalliance.org

Other art groups in town include the Visual Artists Coalition, Sedona Gallery Association, Sedona International Film Festival, Jazz on the Rocks, Sedona Arts Commission, and Northern Arizona Opera League. The Cowboy Artists of America organization was founded in Sedona.

Annual Cultural Events

For a month-by-month list of events, including cultural events, see "The First Steps to the Perfect Trip."

FILM

Sedona International Film Festival This "Top 10" American festival continues to stand out as a success. It is a marvelous chance for locals and visitors to sample the best of the world's independent productions. The Sundance of Arizona has done remarkably well with independent American and foreign movies that won't be showing at the movieplex in your mall. Founded in 1994, it screens more than 100 films. Individual flicks can be viewed for $10 at Harkins Theatres, but day and weekend passes are available. Gala events kick off and close the festival, usually at one of the area's resorts. Someone from Hollywood is sure to be there. The festival is held the last weekend in February. 928-282-1177. www.sedonafilmfestival.com

MUSIC

Jazz on the Rocks If you want to come, make reservations now! Recent celebrities include Chuck Mangione, Diane Shur and Spyro Gyra. Jazz on the Rocks turned 25 years old in 2006. Proceeds benefit music education programs. The festival begins Thursday evening with a fundraising concert, followed by a Friday night concert, a full day of jazz on Saturday, and the jazz brunch on Sunday. Events are held on final weekend in September. Tickets go on sale June 1. Expect to pay approximately $50 for Friday evening, $70 for lawn seating all day on Saturday. Call 928-282-1985. 1487 W. Hwy 89A, Suite 9. www.sedonajazz.com

Sedona Chamber Music Festival This series offers international and U.S. performers. 928-204-2415. www.chambermusicsedona.org

Red Rocks Music Festival This summer offering celebrates classical music and brings fine performers to Sedona. Chamber music and orchestral performances as well as masterclasses and workshops are held throughout the last week of August into Labor Day Weekend. 602-787-1577, 877-733-7257. www.redrocksmusicfestival.com

PAINTING, SCULPTURE, MIXED MEDIA

The Sedona Arts Festival On the second weekend in October Sedona is not an art colony: It becomes an art empire. An immense turnout fills every hotel room in town. The outdoor event features excellent artists from around the country, but the Southwestern focus is naturally the best. Sat-Sun 10am-5pm. $5. Red Rock High School field, W Hwy 89A & Upper Red Rock Loop Road, WS. 928-204-9456. sedonaartsfestival.org

116 **The Sedona Art & Sculpture Walk** This annual tradition features the work of more than 100 sculptors in a special juried event. Although timing and location have changed, the Sculpture Walk has been chugging along for over 17 years. Traditional and innovative materials and styles are showcased, including sculptural works in clay, glass, bronze, wood, marble, neon and found objects. Other fine art mediums include oil, watercolor, acrylics, photography and glass mosaic. The art ranges from small to tall. This event is run by the Sedona Arts Center and in 2006 was held at the end of April at the Radisson Poco Diablo on Hwy 179. 928-282-3809, 888-954-4442. www.sedonasculpturewalk.com

Sedona Plein Air Festival What happens when you gather America's best landscape painters set them loose among the red rocks? You get the outstanding Plein Air Festival, a hit at its inception in 2005. The event takes place the final week of October, with the painters displaying and selling their completed works for sale that weekend at the Sedona Arts Center. 928-282-3809, 888-954-4442. www.sedonapleinairfestival.com

Northern Arizona Watercolor Show This shows presents the works of the Northern Arizona Watercolor Society, whose members paint in one of the world's prettiest regions. This twice-yearly event features the work of up to 20 members. You can meet the artists and purchase original works at this show, typically held in spring and autumn each year. Check

Big Mistake

Visitors looking for beauty and the perfect gift usually miss one of Sedona's great shopping treasures: its art galleries. Now that just about everyone in the gallery business has become retail-savvy, you'll find lovely items in lower prices ranges, even if the bulk of the establisment's art is costly. Plus you'll get to see the beauty and creativity inspired by Sedona's light and color as you shop. So when the malls are crowded, head for the galleries.

with the Sedona Arts Center for information on the society and the show. 928-282-3809, 888-954-4442. www.sedonaartscenter.org

Sedona Arts Center Members Exhibition This juried exhibition showcases member artists and features unique art in a variety of media. Categories include sculpture, ceramics, colored pencil, pastels, oil and acrylic, jewelry, glass, wood, fiber, watercolor and mixed-media. The show gets a good turnout, with a variety of art at a variety of prices. Open to the public for the month of July, 10am–5pm daily. www.sedonaartscenter.org

Sedona Visual Artists Coalition Exhibition Representing approximately 60 of Sedona's best artists, this exhibition is usually held in October. Categories include photography, glass, fiber art, ceramics, mixed media, sculpture and painting.

Sedona Taste You'll find lots and lots and lots of good food and wine at this annual Sedona fundraiser. The shaded grounds by Oak Creek give relief from the heat. It's held the second weekend in June. Los Abrigados Resort. 928-282-7822. www.losabrigados.com

Art Galleries

Nearly all Sedona's art galleries are located along the corridor that winds along Hwy 179 and into Uptown on Hwy 89A. While picking art galleries is certainly a matter of taste, here are 10 that will offer you a diverse and satisfying experience. Personally, I find it interesting that the franchised Thomas Kinkade's idyllic landscapes couldn't make it in this town. The gallery, located in Uptown, closed after a year-long attempt.

10 ART GALLERIES TO LOOK FOR

The Sedona Arts Center At the top of the list is the gallery featuring the art of Sedona's finest local artists. It's the hub of Sedona's visual arts community. Hwy 89A and Art Barn Road, UP. 928-282-3865.

The Eclectic Image Landscape photography is the specialty here, with a focus on Sedona and the Southwest. Tlaquepaque, 336 Hwy 179, BTY. 928-203-4333.

El Prado One of Sedona's oldest galleries is famous for their wind sculptures, visible in their courtyard. Tlaquepaque, 211 Hwy 179, BTY. 928-282-7390.

Exposures This is Arizona's largest gallery, featuring works by prodigy Amanda Dunbar, Southwestern artists Bill Worrell and the Tobeys, and jewelry by Barbara Westwood. 561 Hwy 179, BTY. 928-282-1125.

Kuivato Lots of glass sparkles in this Tlaquepaque store. 336 Hwy 179, BTY. 928-282-1212.

118

Lanning Gallery This contemporary fine art gallery includes oils, acrylics, and watercolors. The playful, large animal sculptures outside are traffic-stoppers. 431 Hwy 179, BTY. 928-282-6865.

Mountain Trails Gallery Here you'll find fine natural sculptures, many by Sedona's most successful artists, Susan Kliewer, Ken Rowe and Ken Payne. Odds are good you'll actually see a sculptor at work. Upstairs in Tlaquepaque. 336 Hwy 179, BTY. 928-282-3225.

Turquoise Tortoise This excellent Southwest-themed gallery features paintings of and by Native Americans. 431 Hwy 179, BTY. 928-282-2262. Also with jewelry in Uptown at Piñon Pointe, 101 N Hwy 89A. 928-282-6018

Visions Fine Art Here is color and lots of it, featuring painters such as the tricky Octavio Ocampo and Thomas Kuebler's humorous sculptures. Piñon Pointe, 101 N Hwy 89A, UP. 928-203-0022. www.visionsfineart.com

Terbush Gallery Dale Terbush's visionary art puts the New Age in paint. Hillside, 671 Hwy 179, BTY. 928-203-4930.

Key Code to Sedona

UP — Uptown
WS — West Sedona
BTY — Below the "Y"
OCC — Oak Creek Canyon
VOC — Village of Oak Creek

Shopping

Ever since tourists have been seeking souvenirs, there have been shops to serve them. The biggest change in the last few years has been the increase in the quality and diversity of stores. Sedona's retail landscape, however, changes quickly. We focus on places that are not only good, but likely to be around by the time you arrive.

119

Here are the most notable areas to do your shopping and a list of our picks in a variety of categories, from practical to fun.

SHOPPING GALLERIAS

Tlaquepaque Built 30 years ago by Abe Miller, Tlaquepaque (tla-keh-pah-keh) is designed to look much older. This is a very pleasant place, inspired by and named for a Mexican artist colony. It has more than 40 specialty shops and art galleries. Classy René of Tlaquepaque restaurant is here, as well as the comfortable Oak Creek Brewery. Best thing about Tlaquepaque? The towering sycamores: They were left in place and the shops built around them. Note that it's tough to find parking on Saturdays and holiday weekends. 336 Hwy 179, BTY. 928-284-4838. www.tlaq.com

Hillside Equally upscale and on the uphill side of the street is a place that Sedonans know because of the lovely lady who built this excellent combination of 15 spots for art, home furnishings, gifts and fashions. It includes the upscale Shugrue's Hillside Grill and the popular Javelina Cantina. Best thing here is the sound of the toads in the little pond on the north side. 671 Hwy 179, BTY. 928-282-4500.

Piñon Pointe Uptown is stretching. Where once upon a time a hillside nestled signs for the local Rotary or Elks Club meeting, now sits the Hyatt and the Piñon Pointe shopping center. The center has art, clothing, gifts, dining and more. Lunch can be taken at Wildflower Bread Company. At the "Y," 1 N Hwy 89A, UP. 928-204-8820.

Uptown Could we leave out Main Street? There's nothing like it. Small enough to walk, but big enough that it is actually hard to walk back and fun to get lost in. You'll see T-shirts, yes, but occasional finds. If you only have limited time to be in Sedona, and you absolutely have to be indoors, then be in Uptown. Favorites include fudge, ice cream, views from Canyon Breeze and the fun of people watching. Within Uptown are mini-malls, including Sacajawea Plaza, Sedona Center and more.

Oak Creek Factory Outlets Looking for bargains? If you're arriving from Phoenix, the outlet mall is one of the first things you'll see. Many of the standard mall brands are here, from Gap to Oneida to Tommy Hilfiger. Best thing about this mall? Shockingly, the food. Find it at The Marketplace Café. 6601 Hwy 179, VOC. 928-284-2150.

120

BARGAIN HUNTING

Art Mart While the quality doesn't always match Sedona's fine galleries, you'll see much lower prices at this large outlet representing local artists. Harkins Theatre Plaza, 2081W Hwy 89A,WS. 928-203-4576.

Outdoor art shows Occasionally throughout the year (especially in spring and autumn), you'll spot open-air art shows in parking lots at Bell Rock Plaza (VOC), Prime Outlet (VOC) and Black Motors (WS).

Dairy Queen In the parking lot next door, low-cost Indian-style jewelry is sold by Navajo dealers. 4551 N Hwy 89A, OCC.

Sedona Trading Post Good selection. 10 Bell Rock Plaza, VOC. 928-284-2555.

STORES, BY CATEGORY

ANTIQUES AND ACCESSORIES

★ **Hummingbird House** This is a charming shop in Sedona's historic Hart General Store. On the corner of Brewer and Ranger roads, accessible from Hwy 89A or Hwy 179 close to the "Y." Custom furniture, antiques, accessories. 100 Brewer Road, BTY. 928-282-0705.

BOOKS

Even if you're not a reader, Sedona's many bookstores are great places to find sightseeing and trail info, meet locals and other visitors, or pick up gifts to take home. In addition to the bookstores listed below, you'll also find good book selections at many Crystals/New Age stores.

The Book Loft Blink and you might miss this interesting second-story shop near the Y. Owners Bob and Valerie have created an old-fashioned bookstore that invites you to stay a while and browse. Shelves are chockfull of new, used and rare books, and reading chairs near the back windows offer magnificent red rock views. Parking is limited. 175 Hwy 179, BTW. 928-282-5173.

Book Warehouse Bargain hunting? Try this store in the Prime Outlet Mall, 6640 Hwy 179, VOC. 928-2824-0042.

Chapel of the Holy Cross Yes, there's a bookstore downstairs, consisting mostly of religious and inspirational texts. End of Chapel Road, off Hwy 179, BTY. 928-282-1622.

★ **Golden Word Book Centre** Located on the far side of West Sedona, this store has a large collection of New Age/spiritual/self-help books and a music listening center featuring over 400 CDs. You'll also find jewelry, fountains and more. 3150 W Hwy 89A, WS. 928-282-1622, 800-248-4405. www.sedonanewagebooks.com

Sedona Books and Music This West Sedona store is popular with locals because of its music selections. No wonder—it's owned by renowned jazz/jazz-fusion guitarist Stanley Jordan. The store also offers instruments and music lessons, as well as a corner devoted to local writers. Located in Bashas' plaza, W Hwy 89A and Coffee Pot Drive, WS. 928-282-5173

★ **Storyteller Books** This very classy shop has a huge selection of local and regional titles as well as bestsellers, gift items and an upstairs book nook for kids. They often host book signings by local authors. Located in Tlaquepaque, 336 Hwy 179, BTY. 928-282-2144.

★ **The Well Red Coyote** This west-side store is owned by mystery writer Kris Neri and her talented musician husband Joe Neri. They offer general books and a good selection of regional titles. They regularly host writing workshops, seminars, book discussions and poetry readings. 3190 W Hwy 89A, WS. 928-282-2284. www.wellredcoyote.com

★ **The Worm** Michael Eich and his staff are known for their friendly and helpful service at this VOC store. Besides books (including local authors and bestsellers), you'll also find an ATM, internet access, newspapers, maps, gift items and more. This is one of the few shops in town that keeps its doors open until 9pm. Factory Outlet Mall, 6645 Hwy 179, Suite C1, VOC. 928-282-3471

CLOCKS

★ **Gordon's** This shop offers lots and lots of clocks and other unique items at a wide range of prices. Hillside Plaza, 671 Hwy 179. 928-204-2069, BTY.

COWBOY BOOTS and HATS

★ **Bob McLean Bootmakers** Items here are custom-made with exceptional craftsmanship. It takes about seven weeks, and the boots will cost anywhere from $650 to $10,000. Hats take a few weeks. 40 Soldier Pass, WS. 928-204-1211.

Cowboy Corral You can walk out of here looking like an extra in a Western film, right down to your boots. 219 N Hwy 89A, UP. 928-282-2040, 800-457-2279. www.cowboycorral.com

Joe Wilcox Stores With seven different locations, this group of stores has Uptown covered. Check out Joe Wilcox Western Wear and Joe Wilcox Stagecoach Emporium for cowboy boots. 928-282-1348, 928-282-1978. www.JoeWilcoxSedona.com

CRYSTALS/NEW AGE

★ **Crystal Magic** An excellent crystal collection is backed by good books, fun clothing, and dustables with a spiritual theme. 2978 W Hwy 89A, WS. 928-282-1622.

Crystal Castle Books, jewelry, music, and other items are offered along with crystals. Two locations: 313 Hwy 179, BTY, 928-282-0698 and 320 N Hwy 89A, UP, 928-282-0653.

Center for the New Age This local landmark has a large collection plus many services. 341 Hwy 179, BTY. 928-282-2085.

Ramsey's Rocks & Minerals Outstanding and knowledgeable service makes this store at the "Y" something special. 152 Hwy 179, BTY. 928-204-2075.

Heartsong New Age Center This west-side store carries crystals, statues, jewelry, books, Aura Soma products and many unusual gift items. There are readers and healers on staff. 3150 W Hwy 89A, WS, 928-282-7089

Sedona Crystal Vortex Here you'll find books, jewelry, music and a great selection of tarot cards and beautiful gift items. Services include aura photography, healings, readings and massage. In the Uptown Mall, 271 N Hwy 98A, 928-282-3543

122

FASHION, MEN'S CLOTHING

West Fork Men's For the "resort casual" look, look here. Hillside, 671 Hwy 179, BTY. 928-204-0088.

FASHION, WOMEN'S CLOTHING

(($)) ★ **Dahling It's You** It's unanimous: Every woman in Sedona likes this store. Find out why. 3004 W Hwy 89A, WS. 928-282-1003. Also in Uptown on west side of Hwy 89A.

Chico's This chain has arrived to good reviews. Piñon Pointe, 101 N Hwy 89A, UP. 928-282-4427.

Erika Morgan New in Uptown, this store offers a "trendy" look. Pinon Pointe, across from Wildflower Bread Co., UP. 928-203-0987.

Favorite Clothing Company Tasteful choices are the focus of this west-side shop. 25 Harmony Drive, WS. 928-282-0995.

Isadora It's all about quality at this small boutique. Tlaquepaque, 211 Hwy 179, BTY. 928-282-6232.

Maria Martin It may be small, but it offers treasures. Piñon Pointe, 101 N Hwy 89A, UP. 928-282-9100.

Ondie Towne USA Leather and off-beat apparel are the themes here. 1155 W Hwy 89A, WS. 928-203-0706.

FURNITURE AND FURNISHINGS

Mexidona 1670 W Hwy 89A, WS. 928-282-0858.
Designs West Home Furnishings 109 Hwy 179, BTY. 928-203-9889.

GIFTS

★ **Environmental Realists** This store features handmade wood items, women's jewelry and nifty little clocks. Tlaquepaque, 336 Hwy 179, BTY. 928-282-4945.

JEWELRY

Geoffrey Roth, Ltd. Tlaquepaque, 336 Hwy 179, BTY. 928-282-7756.
Wayne B. Light Custom Jewelry 3000 W Hwy 89A, WS. 928-282-2131.
Ramsey's Rocks & Minerals Outstanding and knowledgeable service, close to the "Y." 152 Hwy 179, BTY. 928-204-2075.

NATIVE AMERICAN CRAFTS AND JEWELRY

⭐ **Garland's Indian Jewelry** A splendid array of treasures. 3953 N Hwy 89A, OCC. 928-282-6632.

Garland's Navajo Rugs This longtime Sedona family business is renowned for their high-quality rugs, although it may take you many moons to pay the price. 411 Hwy 179, BTY. 928-282-4070.

Hoel's Indian Shop It's a long drive up the canyon, but worth it. Call ahead to make sure the shop will be open for you to view beautiful kachinas and other Native American crafts. 9589 N. Hwy 89A. 928-282-3925, OCC.

Kopavi This second-story shop next to Garland's Navajo Rugs features harder-to-find Hopi jewelry. Hwy 179, BTY. 928-282-4774

ORIENTAL RUGS

Azadi Fine Rugs Hillside, 671 Hwy 179, and Tlaquepaque, Hwy 179, BTY. 928-203-0400.

SOUTHWESTERN CURIOS

⭐ **Son Silver West** I marvel at how they have it all, from signs to salsa to coyote skulls. 1476 Hwy 179, BTY. 928-282-3580.

SPORTING GOODS

⭐ **Sedona Sports** The staff offer lots of free advice. The selection is good in footwear, though you'll find everything from carabiners to bathing suits to yoga togs to canteens. Across from Tlaquepaque, 251 Hwy 179, BTY. 928-282-1317. www.sedonasports.com

Canyon Outfitters This west-side store offers a broad array, with specialties in camping and climbing. It's also good for men's jackets, if you forgot yours. 2701 W Hwy 89A, WS. 928-282-5293.

TOYS

⭐ **Flags, Kites & Fun** The fun never stops, but will the owner give you a ride in his banana yellow convertible? 202 Hwy 179, BTY. 928-282-4496.

⭐ **Sedona Kid Company** I have lots of small nephews and nieces, and all their parents have good taste. They wonder how I find toys that they can't find in any big-city stores. Thanks for making me look good, SKC! 333 N Hwy 89A, UP. 928-282-3571.

What's in a name?

The name "Sedona" seems to be attracting attention. Just think how the following products would have sounded with one of the rejected names for our town such as Schnebly Station, Camp Garden or Bug Jump.

The Sedona Minivan (Kia Corporation)

In 1998 I made one of my few Sedona psychic predictions: a car company would name a vehicle for us. I was hoping for a Mercedes. We got a Kia—a minivan that's lovely to behold…and has the government's highest crash-test safety rating.

Sedona Dinner Club (Las Vegas, NV)

Even tennis stars like Sedona. Andre Agassi and Steffi Graf own this hip restaurant and gambling lounge on West Flamingo Road in Las Vegas, Nevada. Fifteen video poker machines at the bar, and they apparently offer good steaks.

Sedona New Age Shop (Honolulu, Hawaii)

Crystals, gifts, books, aromatherapy, herbs and Feng Shui products, as you would expect. Find it on Ala Moana Boulevard.

The Sedona II Tent (Wenzel Co.)

This two-room family dome sleeps four in an 80-square foot area, with a removable fly, hoop frame and large "D" style door for easy entry/exit. Sale price: $69.99.

The Sedona Hotel Mandalay (Rangoon, Burma)

Facing the city's Royal Palace sit 247 deluxe rooms "graciously designed with an aesthetic eye for both contemporary elegance and traditional grace, and the resplendent Amarapura Ballroom."

6

Taking Care
of Yourself

Alternative Health Centers

Acupuncture and Herbal Medicine This office offers acupuncture and Chinese herbology. 65 Coffee Pot Drive, WS. 928-282-0882.

BR Clinic The Dahn Tao group's newest center is just off the main drag in Uptown. The team emphasizes a holistic approach and hosts a resident physician and acupuncturist. 340 Jordan Road, UP. 928-567-7897.

★ **Therapy on the Rocks** Founder John Barnes is the creator of Myofascial Release, an innovative approach that takes massage to a new level for the evaluation and treatment of pain and dysfunction. When traditional therapy, medication or surgery fail, people head here. 676 N Hwy 89A, UP. 928-282-3002.

Dr James Hutton, NMD Doctor Hutton treats chronic viral, bacterial and antibiotic-resistant infections with auto-hemotherapy, ultraviolet blood irradiation, hydrogen peroxide and Vitamin C infusions. He also does chelation for heavy metal toxicity. 3510 Red Cliffs Lane, WS. 928-203-9013.

Wisdom of the Earth Head to Cornville for the wisdom found in pure essential oils. They offer consultations, seminars and even study-abroad programs in medicinal aromatherapy. 2680 N Page Springs Road, Cornville. 928-649-9968, 888-817-8955. www.WisdomoftheEarth.com

Choices Integrative Health Care of Sedona West meets East at this clinic headed by Devlin Mikles, MD. His staff includes practitioners of acupuncture, Chinese medicine, chiropractic, craniosacral therapy, gestalt, homeopathy, hypnotherapy, physical therapy and other modalities. 2935 Southwest Drive, WS. 877-206-1401, 928-203-4456, 928-203-4497. www.choiceshealthcare.com

Highlight

Sedona is America's alternative healing mecca. The problem is that great individuals can be tough to track. Institutions such as spas and healing centers are a good place to start, but no place has a monopoly on talent. Trust the places we've recommended, then call and ask further to find the right person. The receptionist may not be allowed to answer a direct question like, "Who is best?" But they may be more helpful if you ask, "Who would you go to if you were going to have a session?" "Is there anyone there that people rave about?"

Sedona Center for Complementary Medicine Les Adler, MD, has assembled a team offering acupuncture, chelation therapy, energy medicine, physical therapy, pediatrics, psychology, homeopathy, nutritional counseling, pain management, and many other specialties, all with a holistic approach. 40 Soldiers Pass Rd, WS. 928-282-2520. www.sedonacenter.com

Day and Health Spas

About Face Patricia Wheat offers facials, skin care, body wraps. Signature treatments include a two-hour European Body Facial, Essential Oil Body Wrap and Body Polish as well as a Deluxe European Facial. 450 Jordan Rd, Suite G, UP. 928-203-4076.
Complexions For facials, remember three words: Locals love Lynne. 2155 W Hwy 89A, WS. 928-282-2564.
Mii Amo Enchantment Resort's spa is well-regarded but open only to resort guests. Thinking about staying? See "Where to Stay" for details. 525 Boynton Canyon Rd, WS. 928-282-2900.
★ **New Day Spa** You'll find a warm, restful vibe at this spot. Go all out with the "Body & Soul Reviver," or choose from a number of Ayurvedic treatments. Facials and nail care also available. 1449 W Hwy 89A, WS. 928-282-7502. www.sedonanewdayspa.com
Sedona Rouge The spa of this hotel is open to the public and managed by experienced locals. 2250 W Hwy 89A, WS. 928-203-4842. www.sedonarouge.com
Sedona Spa Visitors are happy with the health club at Los Abrigados Resort. 160 Portal Lane, BTY. 928-282-1777.

Alternative Healing

Missing out on Sedona's alternative healing community would be like going to Italy and not having anything to eat. Décor, design and frills are better in Scottsdale, where people spare no expense to look good. Here, it's all about the healing.

Hair Salons

Salon Virtu Professional team, nice location. Drop-ins welcome. Old Marketplace, 1350 W Hwy 89A, WS. 928-282-1564.
Raymond Rodriguez Salon 2155 Shelby Drive, WS. 928-204-5545.

Health Clubs

Sedona Hilton Spa This well-equipped health club is known to locals as "The Ridge." 10 Ridge View Drive, VOC. 928-284-3800.
Sedona Racquet and Fitness Club This health club features the most tennis courts. 100 Racquet Road, WS. 928-282-4197.
Sedona Spa This busy health club is centrally located at Los Abrigados Resort. 160 Portal Lane, BTY. 928-282-1777.
Radisson Poco Diablo This hotel has a workout room, pool, executive golf course and a couple tennis courts. 1736 Hwy 179, BTY. 928-282-7333.

Hospitals

Sedona Urgent Care This is your first stop for a minor illness or accident care on a non-appointment basis. 2530 W Hwy 89A, WS. 928-203-4183.
Verde Valley Medical Center The area hospital is in Cottonwood, the town 18 miles west of Sedona. 269 S. Candy Lane, Cottonwood. 928-639-6000. The Sedona campus of the facility does take emergencies but often sends them on to Cottonwood, Flagstaff or Phoenix. There is a heli-pad here. 3700 W Hwy 89A, WS. 928-204-3000. A new clinic is opening on the south side of town. 71 Bell Rock Plaza, Hwy 179, VOC. 928-204-4933.

Library

Sedona Public Library The town's library is on the west side, with an annex in the Village of Oak Creek. The main branch has a bank of computers for checking email. 3250 White Bear Road, WS. 928-282-7714. www.sedonalibrary.org

131

Pets

More detailed information about some of these lodgings can be found in "Where to Stay."

PET-FRIENDLY ACCOMMODATIONS
Bell Rock Inn & Suites VOC. $99-$199.
928-282-4161, 800-521-3131.
Best Western Inn of Sedona UP. $75-$150.
928-282-3072, 800-292-6344.
Cathedral Rock Lodge & Retreat Center WS. $150-$165.
928-282-7608, 800-352-9149.
Desert Quail Inn VOC. $69-$159.
928-284-1433, 800-385-0927.
El Portal BTY.
928-203-9405, 800-313-0017.
Forest Houses Resort OCC. $80-$135.
928-282-2999.
Grace's Secret Garden B&B VOC. $125-$150.
928-284-2340, 800-597-2340.
Hilton Sedona Resort & Spa VOC. $150-$485.
928-284-4040, 877-273-3762
Iris Garden Inn UP. $85-$140.
928-282-2552, 800-321-8988.
LaQuinta VOC. $80-$149.
928-284-0711, 800-979-0711.
L'Auberge de Sedona Resort UP. $230-$495.
928-282-1661, 800-272-6777.

The Lodge at Sedona WS. $170-$325.
928-204-1942, 800-619-4467.
Matterhorn Inn UP. $69-$129.
928-282-7176.
Oak Creek Terrace Resort OCC. $82-$225.
928-282-3562, 800-224-2229.
Quail Ridge Resort VOC. $101-$162.
928-284-9327.
Quality Inn King's Ransom BTY. $69-$169.
928-282-7151, 800-846-6164.
Sedona Real Inn WS. $99-$319.
928-282-1414, 877-299-6013.
Sedona Rouge Hotel & Spa WS. $169-$350.
928-203-4111, 866-203-4111.
Sedona Super 8 Motel WS. $59-$109.
928-282-1533, 800-858-7245.
Sky Ranch Lodge WS. $100-$149.
928-282-6400, 888-708-6400.
Sugar Loaf Lodge WS. $45-$73.
928-282-9451, 877-282-0632.
Views Inn VOC. $59-$135.
928-284-2487.
Village Lodge VOC. $39-$89.
928-284-3626, 800-890-0521.
White House Inn WS. $42-$71.
928-282-6680.

PETS, AIRPORT INFORMATION

Phoenix Sky Harbor International Airport in Phoenix is becoming pet-friendly too. "Paw Pad" is the name of the pet park just outside of Terminal 3; while Terminal 4 has the "Bone Yard." These two spots give you and your pet a chance for a water and restroom break. Phoenix Sky Harbor is one of the only airports to offer this amenity to pet owners at no charge. If you're planning to transport your pet via cargo hold, check with airlines regarding restrictions during summer heat. 602-273-3300.

PET SUPPLIES

Bark 'N Purr Pet Care Center They take good care of your pets at Bark 'N Purr. They offer kennels, food and supplies, and grooming. 30 Finley Drive, WS. 928-282-4108. Mon-Fri 8:30am-6:30pm, Sat 8:30am-1pm.

Cody's Pet Emporium Village pets deserve to be pampered too. 6601 Hwy 179, VOC. 928-284-5865.

Three Dog Bakery This bakery for dogs offers fresh-baked dog treats, stocking-stuffers, birthday cakes, boxed snacks and food, as well as unique pet accessories. Sinagua Plaza, 320 N Hwy 89A, UP.

133

PET GROOMING

Classy Critters 2255 Shelby Drive, WS. 928-282-4426.
Bark N' Purr Pet Care Center 30 Finley Drive, WS. 928-282-4108.

VETERINARY CLINICS

Bell Rock Veterinary Clinic 45 Bell Rock Plaza, VOC. 928-284-2840.
Oak Creek Small Animal Clinic 3130 W Hwy 89A, WS. 928-282-1195.
Sedona Animal Clinic 100 Posse Ground Road, WS. 928-282-4133.

Recovery and Support

Alcoholics Anonymous Call 928-646-9428 for details about AA and Al-Anon meeting locations and times. Get information for narcotics, gambling and other 12-step programs via the same number.

Desert Canyon Treatment Center There are good reasons to come to Sedona, and then there are really, really good reasons. The innovative treatment here is focused on addiction recovery, but it isn't a 12 step-approach. The smart, compassionate people at Desert Canyon offer a powerful 28-day program. Shorter outpatient programs are also available. For confidential inquiries and admission information, call 1-888-811-8371. 105 Navajo Drive, WS. 928-204-1122. www.desert-canyon.com

Relocation

Here are a few good numbers to know if you're thinking about moving to Sedona. If you're looking to rent, most people consider *The Red Rock News* (928-282-6888, www.redrocknews.com) the place to begin. This local newspaper comes out on Wednesdays and Fridays. For professional relocation services, go to **J.B. Jochum & Associates** (2155 W Hwy 89A, Suite 213, WS. 928-282-5560, 800-249-6875, www.jbjochum.com).

134

CHAMBER OF COMMERCE

Administrative Offices are at Harkins Theatre Plaza, 45 Sunset Drive, WS. 928-204-1123.
Uptown Visitor Center 331 Forest Road, corner of Hwy 89A. Temporary location; Sinagua Plaza, Upper Level, 320 N. Hwy 89A, Suites 3 and 4, UP. 928-282-7722.
The website for visitors is visitsedona.com; the chamber's official website is www.sedonachamber.com.

RADIO STATIONS

KAZM 780 AM Local news and weather with a mixed program of music and talk.
KQST 102.7 FM Top 40.

RECYCLING

Sedona Recycles 2280 Shelby Drive, WS. 928-204-1185.
www.sedonarecycles.org.
Additonal drop-off site in VOC behind Webers IGA.

SCHOOLS

Arizona is a leader in charter school education, and Sedona boasts some fine boarding schools too. For further private school choices, check surrounding communities.

Pre-school and Public Elementary

Big Park Community School K-8. 25 W. Saddlehorn Road, VOC. 928-204-6500.
West Sedona School K-8. 221 Brewer Road, WS. 928-204-6800.

Pre-school and Charter Elementary

Desert Star Community School A free charter school serving grades K-6, combining Waldorf education and Garner's Multiple Intelligences methods. Good enough for my goddaughter! 928-282-0171, www.desertstarschool.org

Montessori School of Sedona: Pre-school, Montessori approach. 90 Deer Trail Drive, WS. 928-282-4472.

Precious Stones Preschool 390 Dry Creek Road, WS. 928-282-4091.

Sedona Charter School K-8, Montessori approach. 165 Kachina Drive, WS. 928-204-6464,-6486.

Waldorf Red Earth Kindergarten Charity Segal's well-regarded charter is located in West Sedona. 928-204-1221.

135

Private High Schools

The Oak Creek Ranch School This boarding school is located in nearby Cornville. 928-634-5571.

Verde Valley School is a distinguished boarding and day school with an arts and nature focus. 3511 Verde Valley School Road, VOC. 928-284-2272.

Public High School

Sedona Red Rock High 995 Upper Red Rock Loop Road, WS. 928-204-6700.

UTILITIES

Cable Cablevision of Flagstaff (dial area code), 928-774-5336.
Electricity Arizona Power Supply (APS), 928-282-7128
Sanitation Patriot Disposal, 211 Smith Rd, UP. 928-203-9995. Waste Management, 928-282-5411.
Telephone Qwest, 800-244-1111.
Propane AmeriGas, 928-282-4554.
Water Arizona Water Company, 65 Coffee Pot Drive, WS. 928-282-5555.

Weddings

With its tremendous natural beauty, lovely weather and positive energy, Sedona has become the place for many couples to get married or renew their vows. Within the last couple of years, the town has seen an increase in the number of professionals dedicated to making your celebration perfect. In this regard, the **Sedona Wedding Professionals Association** is a great help. From ministers to photographers the many individuals in the business have organized themselves for your benefit, and you can compare descriptions of their services. Check out their website at www.sedonaweddingpa.com

136

Brides and brides-to-be find that Sedona offers a lot of choices for weddings for 50 or fewer guests.

CONSULTANTS and PLANNERS
The planning business offers you many choices. Here are three that have been praised:
Weddings of Sedona Bobbi Moore is highly experienced. 928-300-6448. moore_bobbi@yahoo.com
Sacred Unions Laura Lane's positive attitude, professionalism and personal style make her an excellent planner for your wedding.
Sedona Wedding Planner Karen Lynn is well-organized and friendly. (928) 282-7594, (877) 479-2701. www.sedonaweddingplanner.com

MINISTERS and CEREMONY FACILITATORS
Sedona's independent ministers tend to be more "spiritual" than "religious."
Heart of Sedona Weddings Andrew Murphy, 928-204-5934, 888-808-8919. heartofsedona@esedona.net
All Faiths Sedona Weddings Laurie Reddington, 928-300-9331. laurie@sedonaweddingminister.com
Sedona Minister Ellie Eggart, 928-282-8499, 888-882-8499. info@sedonaminister.com

VENUES and RECEPTIONS

If you're starting small and you'd like a church, begin at the charming **Chapel at Tlaquepaque**, which seats about 40. It can be yours for around $250 and a deposit. A nice package option is to host your guests at René at Tlaquepaque restaurant afterward. Nearby galleries and gardens provide nice spots for shooting photos. Contact Jill Kyriakopoulos. 336 Hwy 179, BTY. 928-282-4838. www.tlaq.com

137

If you need a bigger building for the ceremony, the chapel at the **Verde Valley School** is quaint. VOC, 928-284-2272. For more than 100 people, go with **Church of the Red Rocks**, which has glass on three sides and inspiring views. They're willing to work with people of any Christian denomination, but note that an advance consultation is required. 54 Bowstring Drive, BTY. 928-282-7963.

Outdoor weddings are a nice touch and **Red Rock Crossing** makes a famous backdrop. It costs $7 per car to enter Crescent Moon Ranch, or $5 to buy Red Rock Passes for guests coming in via Verde Valley School Road. This area features a view of dramatic Cathedral Rock and the park attendants are helpful. **Bell Rock** is equally famous for weddings. It has some broad, flatter portions just above its base, if you think you can do a little walking with your wedding dress on. Don't count on the Forest Service to provide information. In fact, don't mention it to them at all. It's a "don't ask, don't tell" thing. Located on Hwy 179 heading north past the Bell Rock Pathway Vista sign.

Your indoor choices are basically the town's major resorts, and these will be more expensive.
L'Auberge de Sedona is a lovely French country inn property by Oak Creek. Their grass lawn set on the hill has a tremendously scenic red rock background. Contact Janeen Freeland at 928-204-4389, 800-272-6777. jfreeland@lauberge.com
Amara Resort in Uptown has created a special lawn and staging area for weddings close to the creek with red rocks high above. www.amararesort.com

Radisson Poco Diablo does a nice ceremony on the golf course. Kara Clark. 928-282-7333, ext. 7434; 800-333-3333. info@radissonsedona.com 1736 Hwy 179, BTY. www.radisson.com/sedonaaz.

Los Abrigados Resort has a lovely lawn by the creek, good for both the wedding and reception. The resort offers plenty of amenities for overnight guests, and the chance to stroll through nearby Tlaquepaque. Audrey Dorfman. 928-282-1777, ext. 7018. adorfman@ilxresorts.com 160 Portal Lane, BTY. 928-282-1777. www.losabrigados.com

Sedona Golf Resort offers you a putting green for a wedding floor and a restaurant at the clubhouse. Janelle Sparkman. 928-284-2093. janelle.sparkman@suncorgolf.com

Across the street at **Hilton Sedona** there's a fine restaurant and plenty of rooms. 1-877-273-3762.

In the warm months, head into Oak Creek Canyon.

Junipine Resort offers a lodgepole gazebo for a creekside wedding, May 1-September 30.

Enchantment Resort doesn't have a clear wedding policy at this time. Call them for details. 525 Boynton Canyon Road, WS. 928-282-2900, 800-826-4180. www.enchantmentresort.com

A few B&Bs also provide opportunities for hosting a wedding. There's the charm of the **Lodge at Sedona** on the west side. Contact Shelley Wachal. 928-204-1942, 800-619-4467. info@lodgeatsedona.com

In Oak Creek Canyon you can have a country wedding at **Briar Patch Inn**. 3190 N Hwy 89A, OCC. 928-282-2342, 888-809-3030. www.briarpatchinn.com

For a unique choice, contact the **Sedona Creative Life Center**, which offers a non-denominational chapel beneath a beautiful spire. Contact Shirley Smith at 928-282-9300. mail@sedonacreativelife.com

REHEARSAL DINNERS

Of course, the resorts above all offer meals. Here are some other ideas for a dinner spot.

Casa Rincon & Tapas Cantina This Mexican restaurant offers private rooms, plus a good place to dance afterwards. Contact Demetri Wagner at 928-282-4849. Demetri@rinconrestaurants.com

Cuccina Rustica/Dahl & DiLuca Both of these Italian restaurants have a lovely ambience. Contact David Dimler at 928-284-3010.

Heartline Café This charming, intimate eating establishment on Sedona's west side has indoor and outdoor seating and delicious food. Contact Phyllis Cline, Deborah Marbach or Diana Wyatt at 928-282-0785. heartline@heartlinecafe.com

139

Page Springs Cellars For a change of pace, let the wine flow in the nearby town of Page Springs. Contact Gayle Diehl at 928-639-3004 or 928-301-5661. gayle@pagespringscellars.com

PHOTOGRAPHERS

You'll have lots of good choices in Sedona, a photographer's paradise. Most offer websites with albums of their work, making it easier to choose a style you like. Here are an upscale choice, and an extremely economical one.

★ **Bob Coates Photography** Bob and his team often do two-camera shoots, increasing your chances of getting all the perfect shots. Professional and with a good sense of humor, Bob can afford to pick who he wants to work with. 928-284-0200, 877-746-8646. www.bcphotography.com

(($)) David Sunfellow Photography David Sunfellow is wonderful guy whose services are so reasonably priced it's a bit shocking. 928-282-6120. weddings@sunfellow.com

VIDEOGRAPHERS

(($)) Sedona Video Productions Tony Sills has lots of experience and reasonable prices. He also offers photographic options. 928-282-4624. sedonavideo@esedona.net

CATERERS

Most of the resorts and restaurants listed above offer catering. For two people who handle it exclusively, consider these.

Rosalie's of Sedona, LLC Bonnie Grant. (928) 204-9060. rosalies@sedona.net

Sweet Jill's Jill Sloan. 928-649-2779. info@sweetjillscafe.com

WEDDING CAKES

Sedona Cake Couture Andrea Blaut has created weddings cakes for Tom Cruise, Kirstie Alley and John Travolta. (I'm pretty sure at least one of them is still married, which is good for Hollywood.) The website offers a lovely portfolio of her successes. 928-204-2887. andrea@sedonacakes.com

Sedona Sweet Arts Formerly known as the Chill Out Bakery. Bakery, wedding accessories and gifts, 2655 W Hwy 89A, WS. 928-282-4635. sedonaweddingcakes.com

FLORISTS

Bliss Extraordinary Floral 928-203-9992. bliss@sedona.net
Mountain High Flowers 928-203-4211, 877-853-3783. mountainhighflowers@msn.com
Sedona Floral & Gifts 928-282-3448, 800-657-0940. sedonafloral@earthlink.net
Show Stoppers 928-203-9096. showstoppers@sedona.net

ATTIRE

Sedona Tuxedos 928-282-7780. tuxedos4u@sedona.net

MUSICIANS and DJS

Harp
Oman Ken 928-204-2725. omanken@yahoo.com
Laurie Riley 928-204-0013. harplaurie@earthlink.net

DJ
Jeanie Carroll 877-283-3969. jc@jeaniecarroll.com
Bobby Russell 866-820-5550. sedonasounds@sedona.net

Flute
Anthony Flesch plays flute (and provides wedding planning services too). 928-204-1872. aflesch@npgcable.com

Guitar
Brian David 928-600-5153, 928-526-3207. kriyaguitarist@aol.com

HAIR and MAKEUP
Fango Hair and Day Spa Salon (928-204-9880, 888-419-0312) and **Chic Hair Salon** (928-282-2475) both provide full service for weddings.

TRANSPORTATION
Sedona Limousines Pre-arranged chauffeuered transportation includes executive sedans, custom vans, or limousines. 928-204-1383, 800-775-6739.

White Tie Limousine Choose a sedan, SUV or van. Wedding rates are $70 per hour and up, depending on vehicle, with a two-hour minimum. Bride and groom receive beverage and fluted glasses as a gift. Vehicle is decorated with ribbons and Just Married signs. Phoenix and Sky Harbor Airport rates (one way) depend on the vehicle. It's $225 for one or two people in the Lincoln Town Car. 928-203-4500. whitetietransportation.com
Luxury Limousine Ride in a white Lincoln Town Car or white Lincoln stretch limousine. 928-204-0620. www.gatewaytosedona.com
Sedona Trolley Worth considering if you'd like transport for your guests. They have up to three trolleys available to take your wedding party out to Enchantment, down to Bell Rock, or just about anywhere in between. 928-282-5400. www.sedona-trolley.com

Worship

Assembly of God, Sedona First Assembly of God
3132 White Bear Road, WS. 928-282-7463.
Baptist (Southern) Crestview Community Church, 1090 W Hwy 89A, WS. 928-282-7405. Village Park Baptist Church, 55 Canyon Diablo Drive, VOC. 928-284-3000.
Bible The Master's Bible Church. 928-282-2155.
Buddhist Kunzang Palyul Choling of Sedona, 3270 White Bear Road, WS. 928-282-5195. Stupa can be seen daily.
Catholic St. John Vianney Catholic Church, 180 Soldiers Pass Road, WS. 928-282-7545.
(There are typically no masses at the Chapel of the Holy Cross.)

Charismatic and Word Solid Rock Church of Sedona, 2301 W Hwy 89A, WS. 928-203-4900.

Christian Science Christian Science Reading Room, 384 Forest Road, BTY. 928-282-3810.

Church of Christ Sedona Church of Christ, 2757 W Hwy 89A, WS. 928-282-7707.

Church of Jesus Christ of Latter-Day Saints Sedona Ward, 160 Mormon Hill. 928-282-3555.

142 **Community and Nazarene** Church of the Nazarene, 55 Rojo Drive, VOC. 928-284-0015. Wayside Chapel Community Church, 401 N Hwy 89A, UP. 928-282-4262.

Episcopal St. Andrew's Episcopal Church, 100 Arroyo Pino Drive, WS. 928-282-4457. St. Luke's Episcopal Church (APCK), Hwy 179, BTY. 928-282-7366.

Hindu 7 Centers Yoga Arts offers kirtan (call-and-response chanting) on Sundays. 2115 Mountain Rd, WS. 928-203-4400.

Interdenominational, Sedona Interfaith Fellowship meets at the Sedona Public Library, WS. 928-282-0293.

Jehovah's Witnesses 110 Northview Road, WS. 928-282-9290.

Jewish Jewish Community of Sedona, 100 Meadowlark Lane, BTY. 928-204-1286.

Lutheran Christ Lutheran Church (ELCA), 25 Chapel Road, WS. 282-1022. Rock of Ages Lutheran Church (Missouri Synod), 390 Dry Creek Road, WS. 282-4091.

Methodist Sedona United Methodist Church, 110 Indian Cliffs Road, BTY. 928-282-1780.

New Age Crystal Sanctuary & Starlight Community Church, 40 Goodrow Lane, WS. 928-282-1146.

Non-Denominational Aquarian Concepts Community, 2120 Hwy 89A, WS. 928-204-1206. Rainbow Ray Focus, 225 Airport Road, WS. 928-282-3427.

Seventh Day Adventist 680 Sunset Drive, WS. 928-282-5121.

United Church of Christ Church of the Red Rocks (Congregational UCC), 54 Bowstring Drive, WS. 928-282-7963.

Unity Unity Church of Sedona, 65 Deer Trail Drive, WS. 928-282-7181.

Wesleyan Christ Center Wesleyan Church, 580 Brewer Road, BTY. 928-282-9767.

(If your denomination isn't represented, check in nearby Cottonwood.)

Yoga

STUDIOS, WORKSHOPS and OUTINGS

Devi Yoga An ashtanga yoga approach is offered by talented teachers Soni and Näthan Gangadean. 9:30am, noon and 5:30pm classes on weekdays, and a 9:30am class on weekends. 215 Coffee Pot Drive, WS. 928-203-4046. www.deviyogasedona.com

7 Centers Yoga Arts The focus is on Hatha and Kundalini yoga at this large center. Daily classes are offered at 8:30am, 10:30am and 5:30pm, and an 8:30am class on weekends. They offer a month-long yoga teacher certificate training several times during the year and host the International Yoga College advanced certification program. With advance notice, this studio also offers private and group outdoor experiences beginning at $75 per hour. 928-203-4400. 2115 Mountain Rd, WS. 928-203-4400. www.7centers.com

Sedona Spirit Yoga Outdoor yoga, retreats and yoga hikes. 928-282-9900, 888-282-9001. www.yogalife.net

143

EASTERN EXERCISES

BR Clinic The Dahn group offers a Korean-influenced series of exercises. 340 Jordan Rd, UP. 928-567-7897.

Key Code to Sedona

UP	—	Uptown
WS	—	West Sedona
BTY	—	Below the "Y"
OCC	—	Oak Creek Canyon
VOC	—	Village of Oak Creek

7

Your Guide to Eating Well

Coffee and Cyber Cafés

Where is the best cup of coffee in town? My crew of caffeine addicts says it isn't Starbucks.

★ **Ravenheart** The new king of coffee added an Uptown location to its west-side HQ. The West Sedona location has the most going on in the evening, with a comfy interior and occasional entertainment. Truffles here are hard to resist. The Uptown shop is for people watching. Both serve shade-grown coffee.
West Sedona (WS) hours: Mon-Sat 7am-9pm, Sun 7am-7pm, Old Marketplace Plaza, 1370 W Hwy 89A, WS. 928-282-5777. Uptown (UP) hours: Mon-Sun 6am-6pm, 206 N Hwy 89A, UP. 928-282-1070.

★ **Sedona Coffee Roasters** This longtime local hangout has the most action in the morning, with a view from the deck. They feature a number of very good blends, including flavored. Mon-Sat 6am-5pm, Sun 6am-3pm. Next to Harkins Theatre complex, 2155 W Hwy 89A, WS. 928-282-0282.

Sedona I-Scream This Village location has high-speed internet services, your computer or theirs. Ice cream too. Mon-Sat 7am-8pm, Sun 10am-8 pm. IGA Shopping Center, 100 Verde Valley School Road, VOC. 928-284-3500.

Starbucks "Couldn't keep 'em out," say some. "Couldn't get here soon enough," say others. It's here, and it's in Uptown. Open daily at 6:30am. Closes at 6:30pm, except for Friday and Saturday, when they close at 8:30pm. Piñon Pointe, 101 N Hwy 89A, UP. 928-204-5580. There's also a Starbucks counter in the Safeway grocery store, 2300 W Hwy 89A, WS.

OTHER WI FI "HOT SPOTS"

The Worm Open 9am-9pm. Factory Outlet Mall, 6645 Hwy 179, Suite C1, VOC. 928-282-3471.
Sedona Library 3250 White Bear Rd, WS. 928-282-7714.
Wildflower Bread Company Piñon Pointe, 101 N Hwy 89A, UP. 928-204-2223.

Breakfast

((($))) Café Jose This west-side spot is a local favorite for early-bird deals and Southwestern breakfasts. Opens at 5:30am. Safeway Plaza, 2370 W Hwy 89A, WS. 928-282-0299.

Coffee Pot This is Sedona's oldest and most famous breakfast spot. If you subscribe to the "When traveling, eat in crowded places" theory, then this is the place to eat. Parking is iffy (you might have to park at the movie theater across the street on a Sunday morning), but you'll have more than 100 omelette choices when you enter. Open 6am-2:30pm. 2050 W Hwy 89A, WS. 928-282-6626.

Desert Flour Bakery Here you can satisfy all your wildest fantasies in baked goods. Mmm! The pastries are splendid. They serve cappuccino too. Open Mon-Sat 7am, 8am on Sundays. 6446 Hwy 179, VOC. 928-284-4633.

New York Bagels & Deli Trust a Jersey boy: These are A+ bagels, fresh with a decent variety. There's lox and plenty of pastries and breakfast sandwiches for more choices, and coffee, of course. Opens daily at 6am. Old Marketplace, 137 W Hwy 89A, WS. 928-204-1242.

The Village Griddle This relaxed, friendly spot serves up one heck of a breakfast burrito and offers plenty of space. Opens at 7am, sometimes earlier in warmer months. Tequa Plaza, 7000 Hwy 179, VOC. 928-284-4123.

Wildflower Bread Company There's a certain appealing crustiness to the bagels, flavorful breads, pastries and tasty breakfast menu options. Opens Mon-Fri 6am, Sat-Sun at 7am. Piñon Pointe Center, 101 N Hwy 89A, UP. 928-204-2223.

UPSCALE BREAKFASTS

Briar Patch Inn Call ahead to see if this B&B is open for visitors. It's especially lovely on sunny summer mornings with live music and the sounds of the creek. 3190 N Hwy 89A, OCC. 928-282-2342, 888-809-3030.

★ **Garland's Oak Creek Lodge** The insider secret for breakfast is definitely this Oak Creek Canyon institution. Up front, I'll tell you that the chances you'll get in are slim. But if they have room, and you'd like something delicious in a great old lodge, call Garland's. In fact, call well ahead and bring an empty stomach for a unique, multiple-course meal that usually includes waffles, eggs, tortillas, or fresh local trout. Order as much as you like for $10-12. Open spring through autumn. Eight miles from Uptown, 8067 N Hwy 89A, OCC. 928-282-3343.

L'Auberge de Sedona You'd expect good French toast from the French restaurant in Uptown, and you'll get it, plus fine service and many other good dishes. This is the class act of breakfast in Sedona. Opens at 7:30am. 301 L'Auberge Lane, UP. 928-282-1661.

148 **El Portal** One of Sedona's finest accommodations offers Sedona's best breakfasts. A steal at $9. 95 Portal Lane, BTY. www.innsedona.com. 928-203-9405, 800-313-0017.

Brunch

Yavapai Restaurant This Enchantment Resort bonanza includes seafood, international cheese pastries, free champagne and light beverages, although you'll still have to pay extra for the espresso. Wanna go really big? Eat in the private sunroom for an additional $250. Sunday, 10:30-2:30pm. $34.50 per adult, $17.25 per child. 928-282-2900.

L'Auberge The buffet includes freshly baked breads, international cheeses and patés, seasonal game, delicate smoked salmon and trout, savory herbed omelettes, pastries and desserts. It's particularly nice to eat at the Terrace on the Creek. Recommended attire is resort casual—no denim, shorts, or athletic attire. Sunday, 11am-3pm. 301 L'Auberge Lane, UP. 928-282-1661.

Briar Patch Inn Call ahead to see if breakfast is open for non-guests. It's especially lovely on sunny summer mornings with live music and sounds of the creek. 3190 N Hwy 89A, OCC. 928-282-2342, 888-809-3030.

Lunch

— FOR A BIG SANDWICH —
(($)) **Sedona Memories** Mike serves up big, big sandwiches. Call in your order for a free cookie. 321 Jordan Road, UP. 928-282-0032.

— LOCAL AND RELIABLE —
Judi's This Sedona institution has good daily specials and some outdoor seating. Baby back ribs stand out among many choices. 40 Soldier Pass Road, WS. 928-282-4499.

— WHERE LOCALS BRING A GUEST —
Heartline Café Delicious food is served in a tasteful atmosphere. 1619 W Hwy 89A, WS. 928-282-0785.

— A SPOT OF TEA —
Taste Café Try the light lunches. Healthy options include free-range meats. 1149 W. Hwy 89A, WS. 928-203-9041.

— THE SHOPPER'S SPECIAL —
The Marketplace Café If you're shopping at the outlet mall, this spot gives "mall food" a much better name. They offer very good grilled vegetable pizza for those who avoid meat. Prime Outlets, 6645 Hwy 179, VOC. 928-284-5478.

— HEALTHY CHOICES —
D'Lish Fast becoming a local favorite, this restaurant serves sit-down vegan and vegetarian meals. Dry Creek Road & W. Hwy 89A, WS. 928-204-2185.

New Frontiers Natural Marketplace Their deli has seating. Old Marketplace, 1420 W Hwy 89A, WS. 928-282-6311.

Rinzai's Grab something wrapped to go. Harkins Plaza, 2081 W. Hwy 89A, WS. 928-204-2185.

Café Bliss and Chocolates (formerly Raw Café) A living gourmet marketplace. 1595 W Hwy 89A, WS. 928-282-2997.

— GREAT VIEWS, LONG DRIVE —
Tii Gavo The best views of all are at Enchantment Resort's grill. Choose from ceiling-high windows indoors or unobstructed majesty outside. It's essential to call ahead, not just for reservations, but to be allowed onto the property. Picks: the balcony, the black bean soup and the nachos. Worth the drive. 525 Boynton Canyon Road, WS. 928-282-2900.

— BEST SALAD AND VIEW COMBO —

Shugrue's Hillside Grill Views are fine indoors by the large windows but even better on the deck. The salad? Try ginger walnut chicken. Reservations are a good idea. Hillside Plaza, 671 Hwy 179, BTY. 928-282-5300.

— BEST DOGGONE VIEW —

Canyon Breeze You can order your food up front by the street, but walk to the back, beyond the bar, for a seat and a view of Snoopy Rock. 300 N Hwy 89A, UP. 928-282-2112.

— OLD WORLD MEETS NEW AGE —

(($)) **Euro Deli** Can Polish sausages and organic vegetables live together in a tasteful new eatery? They're trying over at Euro Deli, where the Stachorskis offer everything from kielbasa to tofu cutlets. Great prices. 3190 W Hwy 89A, WS. 928-282-4798.

— UPTOWN SPECIAL —

Wildflower Bread Company Hard to tell whether more tourists or locals are here. Everyone likes it. They have delicious soups too. Piñon Pointe, 101 N Hwy 89A, UP. 928-204-2223.

— AFTER A HIKE IN OAK CREEK CANYON —

Junipine Café & Grill The best casual dining in Oak Creek Canyon is here—real friendly, real tasty. The shady outdoor patio can't be beat in warm months. Great fish. 8351 N Hwy 89A, OCC. 928-282-7406.

Casual Dining

Ready for dinner? You'll find no lack of choices. But how can you find what you want, where you need it? Here's a Top 10 that covers a broad range of options and locations for you.

A Pizza Heaven This tucked-away location serves up delicious pizza, and very good Italian cuisine choices beyond that. Outdoor seating is available. 2675 W Hwy 89A, WS. 928-282-0519.

The Cowboy Club This well-known place to eat in Uptown offers three levels of Southwestern food and service: the main restaurant, the upscale Silver Saddle room, and the exclusive Red Stone Cabin. 241 N Hwy 89A, UP. 928-282-4200.

Dara Thai Locals consider this small restaurant to have the best Thai food around. Tom Ka Gai soup is a big hit. 34 Bell Rock Plaza, VOC. 928-284-9167.

The Hideaway A good value: Italian food, low prices and outdoor seating above the creek. 251 Hwy 179, BTY. 928-282-4204.

Javelina Cantina You'll find a friendly crowd and tasty margaritas at a convenient location. Fish tacos are a specialty. Outdoor seating is available, with good views. 671 Hwy 179, BTY. 928-203-9514.

Minami Yoshi knows sushi. Across from Prime Outlets, 6586 Hwy 179, VOC. 928-284-0684.

151

Oak Creek Brewery & Grill Nice bar, comfy booths, good location and great beer—try the Seven Dwarfs for a taster. Outdoor seating on the balcony is available. Tlaquepaque, 336 Hwy 179, BTY. 928-282-3300.

★ **Picazzo's** Home of the best casual dining experience in Sedona, Picazzo's presents big salads and addictive pizzas in a stylish, bustling atmosphere. Fair prices, but no reservations are accepted, which means you've got just as good a chance as anybody to get in. Outdoor seating is available, although it is has some street noise. 1855 W Hwy 89A, WS. 928-282-4140.

Red Planet Diner This fun family spot has the best restaurant T-shirt to take home. You'll find aliens, crop circles, reasonable prices, and diner food with an Italian accent. 1655 W Hwy 89A, WS. 928-282-6070.

Takashi This Japanese restaurant has a very pleasant atmosphere, and its location is an easy walk for anyone in Uptown. For this category, a bit pricey. Outdoor seating is available. 465 Jordan Road, UP. 928-282-2334.

Key to Symbols

★ = **Highly Recommended**

((($))) = **Great Value**

Fine Dining

Most guidebooks offer restaurant reviews that boil down to one of two styles. There's the telephone book approach, which lists all the options without giving critical opinions. Then there's the reviewer who strongly suggests one or two spots but leaves you wondering, "How many could he actually have tried?" Here you'll find plenty of options, but with our ratings to help you understand each choice.

How are the ratings determined? First, I interview satisfied and dissatisfied local clients. Second, I check with insiders—the sous chefs and servers, bartenders and managers—asking them to rate their own and other establishments. Third, we have access to written reviews from many, many visitors. And of course, I eat at all of them myself. On food quality, service, ambience and value, these are the restaurants that made the cut.

All five of these restaurants are recommended, and all restaurants recommend reservations. In the spring and autumn high seasons, consider making reservations a day ahead. Each listing is followed by a rating (scale of 1 to 5, with 5 being highest), and its location. Recall that **VOC**=Village of Oak Creek, **WS**=West Sedona, **BTY**=Below the "Y," **OCC**=Oak Creek Canyon and **UP**=Uptown.

By the way, Sedona's general style is more appropriately labeled Casual Fine Dining. Only at the resorts L'Auberge and Enchantment are certain attire restrictions observed. Call them for details.

One final note. The ratings offer general opinions across broad categories determined from lots of meals eaten and served by lots of people. But in Sedona, you're probably having just one meal, and you want it to be great. Perhaps more than any other category, we notice that a fine dining experience is often a matter of feeling. So why not hedge your bets? Enter these establishments anticipating a good time and be grateful for the company of whomever you are dining with…even if it's just you. Chances are, you'll be well rewarded.

THE VERY BEST

Cuccina Rustica   FOOD 3   SERVICE 4   AMBIENCE 5   VOC

This restaurant offers the best ambience in Sedona. If you feel like a million bucks here, it's because that's how much the remarkable interior space cost. Very professional service and a flair for occasions are found here too. The menu offers Italian and Spanish dishes. Entrees $15-$28. MC, Visa, AmEx. Tequa Plaza, 7000 Hwy 179, VOC. www.dahl-diluca.com. (Yes, it's started by the folks who began Dahl & DiLuca.) 928-284-3010.

153

Dahl & DiLuca   FOOD 4   SERVICE 4   AMBIENCE 4   WS

D&D is Sedona's best Italian restaurant and will give you a warm welcome. Good food draws a crowd, so expect a bustling atmosphere. Table for two or table for twenty, it's all good. The Tuscan and Roman meals are kept "fresh and uncomplicated," and the veal dishes are a specialty. Service is generally strong, and there is limited outdoor seating. You can dine to very good jazz music on weekends. Entrees $15-$28. Accepts MC, Visa, AmEx, Disc. 2321 W Hwy 89A, WS. www.dahl-diluca.com. 928-282-5219.

Gallery on Oak Creek   FOOD 5   SERVICE 3   AMBIENCE 4   UP

Amara Resort's restaurant offers Sedona's most interesting menu if you're not afraid of fusion. Asian and Southwestern influences are predominant, and playfully mixed. If you spent your Saturday morning mountain biking, and your afternoon getting a massage, this is the place to enjoy the night. Midweek multi-course specials are a tremendous value. There's outdoor seating with views and music on weekends. Entrees $17-$40. Accepts MC, Visa, AmEx. 310 N Hwy 89A, UP. www.amararesort.com. They could use a better phone system, but try 928-282-4828.

⭐ **René at Tlaquepaque**   FOOD 4   SERVICE 5   AMBIENCE 4   BTY

René is Sedona's best overall restaurant, serving continental cuisine to patrons who appreciate its quiet, elegant feel. Entrees include roasted duck with sun-dried cherry sauce, Rocky Mountain rainbow trout, free-range chicken piccata, Colorado rack of lamb and even a Seitan Wellington for vegetarians. The décor is tasteful, the service is smart and the wine list is excellent. Outdoor seating is in a Tlaquepaque courtyard. Entrees $20-$35. Accepts MC & Visa. www.rene-sedona.com. 928-282-9225.

Shugrue's Hillside Grill   FOOD 3   SERVICE 3   AMBIENCE 4   WS
This reliable restaurant offers classic dishes, classic service and classic views. Views are fine indoors by the large windows and better still on the deck. Sedona's best seafood as well as good meat, poultry and salad choices are served by a professional staff. There's music on weekends. Entrees $22-$32. Accepts MC, Visa, AmEx, DC. Hillside Plaza, 671 Hwy 179, BTY. 928-282-5300.

MORE FINE DINING CHOICES

For those readers who have the luxury of dining often in Sedona, here are more good choices to sample.

Grille at Shadow Rock   FOOD 4   SERVICE 3   AMBIENCE 3 VOC
The Hilton Sedona Resort's restaurant pleases both carnivores and vegetarians. Entrees $15-$28. Accepts MC, Visa, AmEx, Disc. 90 Ridge Trail Drive, VOC. 928-284-6909.

Heartline Café   FOOD 3   SERVICE 2   AMBIENCE 4   WS
Whether you dine inside or out, something about this café feels very…Sedona. Menu changes with the seasons. Their own market is now next door. Entrees $18-$28. Accepts MC, Visa, AmEx, Disc, Diners. 1610 W Hwy 89A, WS. 928-282-0785.

L'Auberge de Sedona   FOOD 3   SERVICE 3   AMBIENCE 5   UP
Elegant French cuisine along lovely Oak Creek. Entrees $27-45. Accepts Visa, MC, AmEx, Disc, Diners. 301 L'Auberge Lane, UP. 928-282-1667.

Reds   FOOD 4   SERVICE 3   AMBIENCE 3   WS
Sedona Rouge's restaurant is like its clients: young and up-and-coming. Entrees $15-$28. Accepts MC, Visa, AmEx, Disc. 2250 W Hwy 89A, WS. 928-203-4111.

Savannah's   FOOD 5   SERVICE 2   AMBIENCE 3   WS
This establishment has excellent cuisine and plenty of choices, as well as a talent for making your occasion special. Entrees $16-$46. Accepts MC, Visa, AmEx, Disc. 2611 W Hwy 89A, WS. 928-282-7959.

Silver Saddle   FOOD 3   SERVICE 4   AMBIENCE 4   UP
Great steaks at this classy but comfortable section of the Cowboy Club in Uptown. Entrees $16-$35. Accepts MC, Visa, AmEx, Disc. 241 N Hwy 89A, UP. 928-282-4200.

154

Yavapai (Enchantment Resort)   FOOD 3   SERVICE 3   AMBIENCE 4   WS
Great views by day, great stars at night. Entrees $26-$42. Accepts MC,
Visa, AmEx, Disc. 525 Boynton Canyon Drive, WS. 928-204-6000.
928-282-2900.

SPECIAL MEALS FOR SPECIAL TIMES
Here's a separate class of establishments that provide fine dining
experiences but are only open part of the week or part of the year.

155

El Portal   FOOD 4   SERVICE 3   AMBIENCE 4   BTY
Sedona's luxury hacienda offers splendid cuisine in an inn setting.
I recommend a drink in the courtyard before beginning Chef Eden's
fresh, varied creations. Entrees $20-$35. MC, Visa, AmEx.
95 Portal Lane, BTY. 928-203-4942, 800-313-0017.

Garland's Oak Creek Lodge FOOD 5   SERVICE 3   AMBIENCE 4   WS
With meals as earthy as Oak Creek Canyon is beautiful, Chef Amanda
Stine pleases guests of the lodge with six or more delicious courses,
including vittles grown in the backyard. The lodge is open from April
through mid-November, and usually full with guests. Call ahead to
get on the waiting list and you may find they've got a spot for you
during your Sedona visit. Cocktails at 6pm, dinner at 7pm. Prix fixe
is typically around $35. 8067 N Hwy 89A, OCC. 928-282-3343.
www.garlandslodge.com. 928-282-2900.

Key Code to Sedona

UP — Uptown
WS — West Sedona
BTY — Below the "Y"
OCC — Oak Creek Canyon
VOC — Village of Oak Creek

Vegetarian and Vegan

DELICATESSENS

New Frontiers Natural Marketplace This large health food store is comparable to the Whole Foods or Wild Oats chains. Daily, 8am-9pm, closes one hour earlier on Sundays. Old Marketplace, 1420 W Hwy 89A, WS. 928-282-6311.

156

Rinzai's Market This small health food store has organic take-out food. Mon-Sat 10am-7pm, closed Sundays. Harkins Theatre Plaza, 2081 W Hwy 89A, WS. 928-204-2185.

EATING OUT

Since Sedona lost The Sage, a popular vegetarian buffet complete with a Tarot deck on each table, many restaurants have taken up the slack. Virtually all Sedona's restaurants have a few vegetarian options on the menu. For a lot of vegetarian choices, try these.

★ **D'Lish** This west-side eatery is an answered prayer for conscious eaters in Sedona. Salads, burritos and various kinds of veggie burgers dominate the menu, but go for the specials whenever you can. 3190 W Hwy 89A, WS. 928-203-9393.

Café Bliss and Chocolates (formerly Raw Café) A living gourmet marketplace. 1595 W Hwy 89A, WS. 928-282-2997.

Thai Spices There's a new and colorful interior, with the same healthy food that west-siders have loved. Macrobiotic choices are available. 2986 W Hwy 89A, WS. 928-282-0599.

Ice Cream and Sweets

ICE CREAM, GELATO, FROZEN YOGURT

The ice cream wars are on with the arrival of a new national chain to take on the locals.

★ **Black Cow Café** They offer a coffee bar, both ice cream and frozen yogurt, juices, draft root beer, and lunch specials. Open till 8pm, in principle. 229 N Hwy 89A, UP. 928-203-9868.

★ **Cold Stone Creamery** Here they don't just serve you a cone. They make it a ceremony. Open till 10pm on Friday and Saturday. Piñon Pointe, 101 N Hwy 89A, UP. 928-203-7700, 274-0083.

Dairy Queen This old reliable is in Sedona's old, reliable Oak Creek Canyon. 4551 N. Hwy 89A, OCC. Open till 7pm during the week, 8pm weekend nights, 9pm summertime. 928-282-2789.

Sedona I-Scream Cyber Cafe The former name may sound more convincing: Sedona Ice Cream Parlour. It's "the" choice in the Village till 8pm. Weber's Plaza, 100 Verde Valley School Rd. 928-284-3500.

CANDY

The candy vortex extends from Uptown to Tlaquepaque.

157

Sedona Fudge Company Any shop that lasts for two decades in Uptown must be good. If you don't want a red dirt T-shirt, try the red dirt candy. You'll find cream cheese, amaretto, raspberry and white chocolate fudge. 257 N Hwy 89A, UP. 928-282-1044.

How Sweet It Is Colorful! Tlaquepaque, 211 Hwy 179, BTY. 928-282-5455.

Rocky Mountain Chocolate Factory Fudge, chocolates, candy apples, assorted candies. Sinagua Plaza, 320 N Hwy 89A, Suite, '0', UP. 928-282-3383.

Grocery/Health Food Stores

Bashas' This popular Arizona chain is just as big as Safeway and noted for a good wine selection. Daily, 6am-11pm. Bashas' Plaza, 160 Coffee Pot Drive, WS. 928-282-5351.

Indian Gardens Trading Post Your Oak Creek Canyon option also has a deli. Summer: Daily, 8am-6pm, Friday and Saturday till 7pm. Winter: Sun-Mon 8am-4pm, Wed-Sat 8am-6pm. Closed Tuesdays. 3951 N Hwy 89A, OCC. 928-282-7702.

New Frontiers Natural Marketplace This large store has a healthy focus and an extensive vitamin and supplement section. Daily, 8am-9pm, closes one hour early on Sundays. Old Marketplace, 1420 W Hwy 89A, WS. 928-282-6311.

★ **Rinzai's Market** Small, but somehow this store has it all when it comes to healthy foods. They also sell vitamins, supplements and offer helpful health consultations. Mon-Sat 10am-7pm, closed Sundays. Harkins Theatre Plaza, 2081 W Hwy 89A, WS. 928-204-2185.

Safeway Food & Drug This large national chain now has an organic line. Daily, 5am-11pm. Safeway Plaza, 2300 W Hwy 89A, WS. 928-282-0118.

Weber's Food & Drug This is the largest market in the Village of Oak Creek. Daily 6am-10pm, closes one hour early on Sundays. 100 Verde Valley School Road, VOC. 928-284-1144.

Wine

VINEYARDS, WINERIES and UNUSUAL OPTIONS

OPTION 1
VISIT A VINEYARD

Page Springs Vineyards & Cellars Owner Eric has no airs about him, except for the lovely aromas floating up from the wines. They specialize in Rhone-style wines. 1500 N Page Springs Road, Cornville. www.pagespringscellars.com. 928-639-3004.

Oak Creek Vineyards & Winery Chardonnay, Fumé Blanc, White Zinfandel, Merlot, Syrah and Zinfandel grapes bask proudly on terraced slops directly across from Oak Creek. Wed-Sun, 11am-5pm. Across from the Page Spring Fish Hatchery on Page Spring Road, Cornville, off of Hwy 89A. 928-649-0290.

OPTION 2
RIDE THE TRAIN, GET A TASTE

Verde Canyon Railroad Each summer, this railroad tour turns into a "Grape Train Escape." The Verde Canyon is pretty, and wine tasting can be enjoyed as you view it. Hwy 89A through Cottonwood past the Tuzigoot entrance. 300 North Broadway, Clarkdale, AZ. 800-320-0718. www.verdecanyonrr.com.

OPTION 3
BUY A MEMBERSHIP

Echo Canyon Vineyards Entrepreneur John Markus has started his own winery and invites you to join the "Fortunate 500" wine club. This boutique vineyard won an American Wine Society Award in 2005. They say the cool nights and volcanic soil are the secret. www.echocanyonwinery.com. 928-634-8122.

WINE and GOURMET FOODS

A'Roma Why does everyone in the Village of Oak Creek look happy? They're eating better! Located two doors down from wildly popular Cuccina Rustica is Lisa Dahl's latest venture, offering gourmet lunches to go, wine, desserts and deli choices. Tequa Plaza, 7000 Hwy 179, VOC.

The Art of Wine Wine tasting is offered every day in this Uptown store. Open daily, 10am-7pm. Piñon Pointe, 101 N Hwy 89A, 928-203-9463.

Heartline Café Market The west-side gourmet market captures the good taste of the neighboring restaurant. 1600 W Hwy 89A, WS. 928-282-0785.

WINE TASTING AT RESTAURANTS

Savannah's and Amara Resort's **Gallery on Oak Creek** are two local spots offering frequent wine-tasting dinners. **Yavapai Restaurant** at Enchantment Resort offers day-time wine tasting sessions each week.

8

Having Fun Once the Sun Goes Down

After Hours

Olde Sedona This west-side establishment offers entertainment and a food menu at the bar after the restaurant closes at 9pm. Open until 2am. 1405 W Hwy 89A. 928-282-5670.

Steak & Sticks Steers, cigars and billiards. Los Abrigados, 160 Portal Lane, BTY. 928-204-7849.

Bar and Club Scene

Where's the action at night in Sedona? The answer seems to change, but for starters, let's go to the west side of town. **Relic's**, a renovated restaurant, bar, dance hall and antiques shop was once known as Rainbow's End. The dance hall now has dinner tables, but the stage is still there for music. The fun, however, is by the bar and billiards or outside on the covered patio, which is especially nice in warmer months. **Olde Sedona** is a restaurant and bar with a past, having changed hands and names several times. It's okay: This town supports reincarnation. Olde Sedona has introduced a menu of good food at reasonable prices, and plenty of video screens in case the music doesn't appeal. On warm evenings, you can hang out on the roof. Live music is on tap most of the week.

While martini bars, wine bars and discos have come and gone, things are just as they've always been at the **Oak Creek Brewery**. You'll find mountain bikers and motorcyclists discussing the beauty of their red rock rides that day. This is an excellent micro-brewery, with a covered patio and bands on many nights, drumming on Wednesdays.

Red Planet Diner has big screens if you need a west-side sports spot. (Go, Diamondbacks!) Also on the west side is the **Sundowner** if you just want to drink without the frills.

The Uptown hangout is clearly **The Cowboy Club**. The long bar by the restaurant hosts wedding parties staying at L'Auberge, tourists passing through, and jeep tour drivers who need a tall drink of water.

Just below the "Y" off Hwy 179, Los Abrigados resort hosts **Steak & Sticks**, the best place for billiards and a spot open till 1am, later than most. There's a nice fireplace to sit by, but the smoke is from cigars. Located at Los Abrigados (on Hwy 179, one-third mile south of the "Y"), it generally draws in timeshare guests at Los Abrigados, and timeshare salesmen from town. Its neighbor, **On The Rocks Bar & Grill,** gets the sports crowd, and will be full of fans of whichever pro sports team is playing that night. Just across the parking lot is **Oak Creek Brewery & Grill** at Tlaquepaque. This place is more upscale than its west-side sibling, and is a better retreat if you've just dined out in style. The brewery's food goes well with its fine beers, and the bartending is great.

163

Big Mistake

Whatever you do, never ask the locals about Sedona's nightlife. They'll laugh out loud and insist there is none. Why? First, they forget that the area hosts lots of non-traditional events at night. Second, most are unaware of new additions and weekly events. Third, nowhere in the world are great artists more underappreciated than in their own home towns. Instead of asking the locals, check out the weekly event guides *Kudos* and *The Scene* (produced by the *The Red Rock News*), the monthly *Red Rock Review,* and the bimonthly *Four Corners.*

Is there life in the Village? Sedona's southern side offers an expanded **PJ's Village Pub**. They now offer entertainment and food to go with the bar selections. Live bands play on weekends. There's a nice look to **The Full Moon Saloon**, which has become an institution in the back of the Tequa Plaza. It is next best in the Village, with a pleasing layout including bar, lounge and small stage. **The Marketplace Café** has a bar and weekly jazz music. I wouldn't call the nightlife "hot" at **Mulligan's**, the restaurant/bar for the Oakcreek Country Club, but it does host events on occasion in the back room. **Hilton Sedona** has a bar at its restaurant, **The Grille at Shadow Rock**. As soon as something happens there, we'll tell you. If you're looking for action, you're better off walking down to **Full Moon Saloon**.

The **Spirit Room**, located in Jerome, is a bit of a drive but a helluva good time if you ride in on your Harley. It's like the sixties all over again. Jerome is about 30 minutes west of Sedona.

The Cowboy Club 241 N Hwy 89A, UP. 928-282-4200.

Full Moon Saloon Tequa Plaza, 7000 Hwy 179, VOC. 928-284-1872.

Hilton Sedona 90 Ridge Trail Drive, VOC. 928-284-4040.

The Marketplace Café Prime Outlets, 6645 Hwy 179, VOC. 928-284-5478.

Mulligan's 690 Bell Rock Boulevard, VOC. 928-284-3687.

Oak Creek Brewery 2050 Yavapai Drive, WS. 928-204-1300.

Oak Creek Brewery & Grill Tlaquepaque, 336 Hwy 179, BTY. 928-282-3300.

Olde Sedona 1405 W Hwy 89A, WS. 928-282-5670.

On the Rocks Bar & Grill Los Abrigados Resort, 160 Portal Lane, BTY. 928-282-1777.

PJ's Village Pub 40 Cortez Drive, VOC. 928-284-2250.

Red Planet Diner 1655 W Hwy 89A, WS. 928-282-6070.

Relic's 3235 W Hwy 89A, WS. 928-282-1593.

The Spirit Room 166 Main Street, Jerome. 928-634-8809.

Steak & Sticks Los Abrigados Resort, 160 Portal Lane, BTY. 928-282-1777.

The Sundowner 37 Navajo Drive, WS. 928-282-1858.

Highlight

With an increasing number of special events throughout the year, one of the coolest ways to see the Sedona scene is to check out the festival parties. Coming at the start and finish of festival weeks, you'll find them for jazz, chamber music, the film festival and fine art shows. They may cost a bit, but they're a wonderful way to meet the artists, as well as hobnob with Sedona's cultural elite.

Bowling

Shake, Rattle & Bowl This alley is located within Cliff Castle Casino on the Yavapai-Apache Reservation. Johnny Rocket's, also in the casino, offers late-night eats. Head south 30 minutes on I-17 to exit 289. 928-567-7950.

Comedy

The best successes in humor have come in the realm of improvisation, where troupes take the stage and perform in response to your suggestions. Two local troupes take the stage fairly regularly in town. Check with your innkeeper or concierge for their current performance schedule, or call the numbers listed below.

Abandoned Minds This large troupe performs both short and long-form improvisation. Directed by Kerry Biondo, their usual venue is the Sedona Community Center. 928-204-0089, 928-821-4302.

Divine Improvidence Although they have performed in Toronto, Las Vegas and New York, this funny foursome calls Sedona home. From social satire to commentary about relationships and politics, they deliver improvised comedy that both locals and visitors enjoy. Uncensored, it may not be ideal for kids. Ask your concierge for venue and time, or call 928-284-0935. www.DivineImprovidence.com

Gambling

Cliff Castle Casino This casino is much closer than Las Vegas, but not exactly next door, as it's located on the Yavapai-Apache reservation. The Dragonfly Lounge has weekly entertainment, and each week-night is appointed for comedy, karaoke, etc. Head south 30 minutes on I-17 to exit 289. 928-567-7660.

Happy Hours

Cuccina Rustica You don't have to wait until dinner at the restaurant with the best ambience in town. Great for sunset, with low-priced, very tasty appetizers. Tequa Plaza, 7000 Hwy 179, VOC. 928-284-3010.

Javelina Cantina Imbibe tasty margaritas in a fun atmosphere. 671 Hwy 179, BTY. 928-203-9514.

Picazzo's Come here for a good time, and meet locals such as the realtor, the psychic, and the psychic realtor. Many Sedonans still refer to it by its original name, Pizza Picazzo. 1855 W Hwy 89A, WS. 928-282-4140.

Reds A hip happy hour for the three categories that are hard to find in Sedona: young, urban and professional. Sedona Rouge Hotel & Spa, 2250 W Hwy 89A, WS. 928-203-4111.

Ice Cream

Black Cow Café They offer a coffee bar, ice cream and frozen yogurt, juices, draft root beer, and lunch specials. Nothing beats a cone and a stroll in Uptown. Open till 8pm, in principle. 229 N Hwy 89A, UP. 928-203-9868.

Cold Stone Creamery Your best late option. Open till 10pm on Friday and Saturday. Piñon Pointe, 101 N Hwy 89A, UP. 928-203-7700, 274-0083.

Dairy Queen This old reliable is in Sedona's old, reliable Oak Creek Canyon. 4551 N Hwy 89A, OCC. 928-282-2789. Open till 7pm during the week, 8pm weekend nights, 9pm summertime.

Sedona I-Scream Cyber Cafe Formerly the Sedona Ice Cream Parlour, it's still the choice in the Village. Open till 8pm. Weber's Plaza, 100 Verde Valley School Road. 928-284-3500.

Liquor Stores

Drug stores, convenience markets and large grocery stores including Bashas' (WS), Safeway (WS) and Weber's IGA (VOC) sell alcohol.
C-Market Jordan Road and 89A, UP. 928-282-4014
Sedona Liquors 122 Hwy 179, BTY. 928-282-7997
Top Shelf Liquors 1730 W Hwy 89A, WS

167

Movies and Videos

MOVIE THEATER
Harkins Sedona 6 Luxury Cinemas Want to catch a flick? With six screens, you can expect current films to be playing here. It's a primary venue for the Sedona International Film Festival. Harkins Theatre Plaza, 2081 W Hwy 89A, WS. 928-282-0222. www.harkinstheatres.com

VIDEO STORES
Movie Gallery Safeway Plaza, 2370 W Hwy 89A, WS. 928-282-5100
It's Movie Time IGA/Weber's Plaza, 100 Verde Valley School Road, VOC. 928-284-5555.

Highlight

The Sedona Gallery Association now offers "First Friday - Evening in the Galleries." This monthly event features the finest galleries and artwork in Sedona. Participating galleries stay open late and host special events and openings the first Friday of every month. Stop by the Visitors Center in Uptown for a map of the galleries.

Music

WHERE TO HEAR IT

Cliff Castle Casino's Stargazer Pavilion hosts acts touring the nation. 928-567-7999.

Oak Creek Brewery This casual venue has bands on the weekends and some week nights. It's also home of the most wicked drumming jam on Wednesdays. Bring anything you can drum. 2050 Yavapai Drive, WS. 928-204-1300.

Olde Sedona There's just enough room to dance in front of the band. New ownership appears dedicated to bringing in good entertainment. 1405 W Hwy 89A, WS. 928-282-5670.

Relic's Formerly known as Rainbow's End. This spot offers restaurant, bar and billiards. The covered patio is fine for fun on warm nights. 3235 W Hwy 89A, WS. 928-282-1593.

Sedona Creative Life Center In sharp contrast to the clubs and cantinas mentioned above is this venue for concerts, workshops and lectures. The main room offers a good stage, but you won't be dancing as you watch. There's no food or drink here, just rows of chairs on a carpeted floor. 333 Schnebly Hill Rd, BTY. 928-282-9300.

LOCAL PERFORMERS

A number of restaurants often have an individual or pair as background music. These include **Dahl & DiLuca**, **Shugrue's Hillside Grill**, **Javelina Cantina**, **Savannah's** and **Relics**.

While there may be a lack of performance spaces, there's no lack of performers to fill them. If you didn't arrive for the Jazz on the Rocks festival, you can still get plenty of jazz. **Bobby Cottonwood**, **Les Zimmler** and **Walt Fluory** are frequently heard jazz pianists, and **Vismaya** is the sultry Swedish singer you'll be lucky to hear.

Thinking more of dancing to the hits? **Sammy Davis** and his band won't quit until you start dancing. **Danny Rhodes and the Messengers** are professionals who play rock and blues. **The Groove Kittens** are fun and lively, with a pop and country focus. The talented members of **Radio Dogma** cover alternative hits and play tunes of their own.

Sedona is lucky to have many outstanding guitarists. **Stanley Jordan** is innovative and highly entertaining, so much so that he tours frequently: if he's playing in Sedona, it's a must-see. **William Eaton** has an equally unique approach. He often appears with Native American fluteplayer Carlos Nakai and shows off his hand-crafted guitars, lutes and other instruments of pure imagination.

Scott Beck plays frequently in the area, and young **Seith (Näthan) Gangadean** may be discovered by time you get here. Both **Robin Miller** (rock-and-roller side, New-Age side) and his son **Eric Miller** perform, although not often together. **Fitzhugh Jenkins** is splendid to hear, when you can find him, usually with talented **Zirque Bonner** on keyboards as part of the **Jazz Bedouins**. Singer/songwriter **Vyktoria Pratt Keating** has a lovely voice and great stories, as does Dutch import **Simone Awhina**.

169

Michelle Branch is our home-town success; she's now a pop queen in rotation on MTV. Next most notable is New Agey **Chris Spheeris**, the Yanni of Sedona. His concerts are highly popular. **Jesse Kalu** is a fluteplayer in the Native American/New Age tradition. He plays regularly on Friday, Saturday and Sundays for an hour in a wonderful and uplifting performance.

Poetry

Poetry? Yes, poetry! **Christopher Lane** and other members of the Northern Arizona Poetry Community (NORAZ) can be heard in entertaining readings, open mic nights and competitive poetry "slams" staged around the area. **The Well-Red Coyote** (Hwy 89A, WS) is a frequent stage, but look for them to return to the theater stage... as soon as the town gets one. Poetry events hotline: 866-698-8790. www.norazpoets.org

Sports Bars

On the Rocks Bar & Grill This spacious bar has plenty of food. Los Abrigados Resort, 160 Portal Lane, BTY. 928-282-1777. For a pool game, head through the side doors into **Steak & Sticks**.
Olde Sedona This restaurant has a good menu and a nice flat-screen TV in the bar. 1405 W Hwy 89A, WS. 928-282-5670.

Stargazing

To do some stargazing on your own, drive up to **Airport Mesa**. At the overlook (right-hand side as you crest the mesa) you can watch the glimmer of town below and the stars above. Bonus: It's an excellent make-out spot. Alternatively, cruise slowly on **Dry Creek Road**, off W Hwy 89A. Although Sedona doesn't have much ambient light, there's even less just a mile out of town. Bring a flashlight because you don't want to hit a cactus when you were aiming for **Bell Rock**. The stretch between here and the Chapel of the Holy Cross, lit up in the distance, is dark and vacuous. Star-gazing here is positively other-worldly.

Evening Sky Tours Enjoy an entertaining evening of astronomy in Sedona. Guides will bring their telescopes to your hotel, or you can meet them at their out-of-town spot. This 90-minute show costs $60 per person for less than four people, $45 per person for five or more people, $20 per child, group discounts. Yes, you'll get your money back if it is too cloudy to see. 1-866-701-0398. 928-853-9778, 866-701-0398.

Key to Symbols

★ = **Highly Recommended**

((($))) = **Great Value**

Theater

How does it feel to be a thriving arts community and yet not have a theater? Embarrassing. Sedona's beloved Canyon Moon Theatre is currently between locations. 928-282-6212. www.canyonmoonthreatre.org Here's what is available:

★ **Shakespeare Sedona** The bard's works go up when the sun goes down. Plays are usually held at Tlaquepaque and sometimes at Red Rock High School. Shakespeare Sedona also features talented teachers from around the country who offer an excellent institute to train actors in the classical tradition. Both the performances and the classes are held in July. 800-768-9286. www.shakespearesedona.com

Blazin' M Ranch Western Dinner Theater If Shakespeare is on one end of the scale, this is the other. For country and corny, head for this chuckwagon supper and show. 1875 Mabery Ranch Road, Cottonwood. 928-634-0334, 800-937-8643.

Future Studios This performance space showcases independent movies and troupes performing music and dance. 30 Hozoni Drive, WS. 928-203-4080.

Wine Bars

The Art of Wine Wine tasting continues daily until 7pm. Piñon Pointe, 101 N Hwy 89A, UP. 101 N Hwy 89A, 928-203-9463. Call regarding new VOC location.

9

Beyond the Red Rocks

Jerome

PLANNING THE VISIT

At a mile high in altitude, the former ghost town of Jerome offers lovely views of the Verde Valley and cooler temperatures than Sedona. If you've never been to either Sedona or Jerome, take a moment to figure out the value of a side trip to this interesting spot. Jerome is not a smart choice if you've only got a weekend in Sedona. There is simply too much to see and do in Sedona to spare the time to see Jerome. I recommend you spend a full three days in Sedona before you consider the trip.

There are three exceptions to this advice. First, if you lack the mobility to enjoy Sedona's outdoors on foot, Jerome provides scenery via the drive. Second, if you are particularly interested in the history of the Old West, Jerome has one heck of a good tale to tell. Third, if you're here on a Harley, then Jerome is calling you.

If you've got a week to stay in Sedona, you could spend a full day in Jerome and the neighboring towns. I'd add a little time at the Tuzigoot ruins, a visit to Old Town Cottonwood or the Verde Canyon train ride from Clarkdale. Alternatively, you could make Jerome a stop on your way back to the airport in Phoenix, returning via Cottonwood or taking a longer trip through Prescott.

INTRODUCTION and HISTORY

To make the most of a visit to Jerome, make the minor effort to see the excellent movie shown at the **Douglas Mansion**, which is now a state park. (Start times for the movie are impossible to predict. Their system? They begin when the first person of the day asks, "May I see the movie?" and run about every 25 minutes after that.) After you've enjoyed the movie, the following suggestions will fit in nicely. If you pass on the movie, you'll have no idea what it is you are seeing.

The reason is that Jerome, like other ghost towns, is all about what was. And what was in Jerome was something remarkable. The United Verde Copper Company began mining the hillside and named the town for Eugene Jerome, long-distance financier of the venture.

174

That company folded in just two years, thanks to high transportation costs. A new owner named William A. Clark had a better go at it, and by the early 1900s, Jerome was the center of action in these parts, home to the largest copper-producing mine in the territory, as well as everything from an opera house to a brothel.

In 1929 Jerome's population reached a staggering 15,000 people, many of whom helped it become one of the world's wealthiest copper camps. After the stock market crash, however, the price of copper dropped through the floor. By 1932 the United Verde Mine closed and the once-rich vein of the Little Daisy Mine followed in 1938. Jerome became a ghost of its former self and remained so for years.

In the 1970s population grew again when Jerome became a hippie haven. Legend has it that in 1979 the entire town was arrested, including the mayor, for growing "an illegal agricultural product." The last quarter century has seen an influx of artisans and art retailers. Tourists in tour buses and riders on Harleys find Jerome a place of dramatic views and fascinating history. Today, this registered National Historic Landmark is home to about 500 citizens.

BUILDINGS and ATTRACTIONS

Douglas Mansion Built in 1916 on a hill just above the Little Daisy Mine, this home is now a state park with exhibits on the town's connection to Winston Churchill, various minerals unearthed during mining and the many miles of underground shafts and tunnels. There are picnic tables outside. Arriving on Hwy 89A, turn right on Douglas Road as you wind uphill toward the town. 928-634-5381.

Mine Museum This storefront museum is an interesting spot to continue investigating Jerome's mining history. Located close to the central intersection.

The Sliding Jail The town's former jailhouse keeps moving. Literally. It's located by the scenic parking lot as you enter the heart of town.

Gold King Mine You can visit this mine a mile to the north. Look for signs and don't be surprised if you see one that says "Haynes, Arizona." This was once considered a separate town. There are old cars, old tractors and old mules to see.

PLACES TO EAT

The Asylum Further up the hill and inside the Grand Hotel, a former hospital, this may be Jerome's best restaurant. 200 Hill Street. 928-639-3197.

The Haunted Hamburger This is a fun place to grab some good food. Aim for the back porch to get superior views. Just above and to the left of the town park. 410 North Clark Street. 928-634-0554.

Flatiron Café This is a good lunch spot on the corner heading downhill.928-634-2733.

PLACES TO SHOP

Nellie Bly There are a number of art galleries in Jerome, but for curios, try this shop. 130 and 136 Main Street.

GOOD TIMES

The Spirit Room This saloon on the main drag acts as Fun Central in Jerome, and it's the place to park your Harley. No kidding: The town becomes Hog Heaven on the weekend, when motorcyclists cruising through the Southwest drop in to hear good ol' rock and roll. 166 Main Street.

DRIVING TIME and DIRECTIONS

Follow Hwy 89A west from Sedona. Two miles into Cottonwood, look for the left-hand turn lane at the stoplight. You have two choices: Turn left for the cut-off road to Jerome or continue to Old Town Cottonwood and Clarkdale, where you will turn left onto Hwy 89A to Jerome.

From the Village of Oak Creek, you can also drive south on Hwy 179 to the Beaverhead Flats Road. It is a right-hand turn off Hwy 179, and takes you through Cornville and past the Verde Santa Fe golf course. Turn left onto Hwy 89A at the intersection and continue through Cottonwood as mentioned above.

Hwy 89A winds sharply as you head up to Cleopatra Hill and the town. You'll see signs for the Douglas Mansion on the right. The town center is further ahead, and there is public parking. The small Chamber of Commerce Visitor Center is next to the lot. Jerome is small enough that you can get out and walk almost everywhere you need to go, except for the Douglas Mansion. However, it is hilly and the air is thinner.

The drive from Sedona to Jerome is approximately 35 minutes. If you continue on Hwy 89A, you'll climb up and over Mingus Mountain, then down to the valley surrounding Prescott, Arizona. This would be a long, scenic route back to Phoenix, if you have the time and inclination to explore.

177

Grand Canyon

INTRODUCTION

President Theodore Roosevelt once called Grand Canyon "the place every American should see." With five million visitors a year, it seems we're all trying. If you're planning to visit Grand Canyon as a day trip from Sedona, consider the following.

Staying in Sedona does make sense because it saves you nearly four hours, round-trip, versus visiting the Grand Canyon from Phoenix or Las Vegas. If you're taking one day for the canyon, four hours makes a big difference. However, I've known many visitors who spent more time at the canyon than at Sedona, and universally, they were disappointed. Given the canyon's reputation, I know this sounds crazy, but the canyon is difficult for the average traveler to exploit. Trails into the canyon are very steep, and most of the rim trail above is flat. Frankly, people get bored or turned off by the rim crowds.

If you're not doing a river trip or an extended camping adventure, the best way to see Grand Canyon, in my opinion, is to stay for one night. That gives you the advantage of seeing the canyon during sunset and/or sunrise hours, when it is most spectacular. It also gives you the chance to avoid the mid-day crowds on bus tours from Phoenix and Las Vegas.

If, however, you need to see the Grand Canyon in one day, beginning and ending at Sedona, this section is for you. Below are nine options for the day trip.

PLANNING THE DAY

Begin with the end in mind. First, ask yourself a few questions: What time do we need to be back in Sedona? Will we dine in Sedona? Do we want to stay for a Grand Canyon sunset? How do we feel about driving in the dark?

Second, consider that the canyon region holds many treasures. Yes, there are the views at the canyon itself, but there are also ancient ruins, geological features and modern native cultures to explore on the way. Would you rather hike or shop or float in a raft, fly above the canyon or dine by the rim? Are you willing to drive to see more, or are you looking for a speedy visit? What value does having a guide mean to you?

Of course, you didn't buy this guide book for questions: You're expecting answers. Here they come.

Keep a few factors in mind. Each day, in addition to you, there may be ten thousand people coming from the Phoenix and Las Vegas areas to see the Grand Canyon too. The good news is that you've got a considerable head start on them, as their trip will take at least four hours each way. By the shortest route, yours will take two hours and 15 minutes. Keep in mind that temperatures are 10 degrees cooler (and much cooler at night), and winter driving conditions can be challenging.

Option 1
On Your Own: Getting There Quickly

This is the choice for people who prefer driving on their own and want to get to the canyon quickly. Also, if your greatest desire for the day is to hike in the canyon, take this route to get there fast, and therefore have the maximum possible time for walking.

Follow Hwy 89A north through Oak Creek Canyon. Twenty-eight miles north of Uptown, you'll see signs for I-17. Turn right onto the highway overpass and left to head north on I-17. From I-17 take I-40 west (toward Los Angeles) to Williams, Arizona. Exit at Hwy 64, taking it north to Grand Canyon.

OPTION 2
ON YOUR OWN: SCENIC/CULTURAL ROUTE

Travelers who want to see not only the big hole in the ground, but also the processes that built it and people who surrounded it should consider this route. Travelers with a full day at their disposal and travelers who want to avoid crowds will like this way best. This route shows you ancient ruins and Navajo trading posts, not to mention a volcano.

Fill up the tank the night before and be on your way no later than 9am. Leave Sedona via Hwy 89A through Uptown and Oak Creek Canyon. This route is quicker and lovelier than I-17. Along the way, you'll cross Midgley Bridge, with a nice look at Wilson Mountain to your left, Sedona's highest peak.

Several miles ahead on the left, you'll see **Garland's**, the oldest retail store in the area, renowned for its Native American jewelry collection. Seven miles along, you'll pass **Slide Rock State Park**, the place to beat the heat in the summer. At about 10 miles, you'll notice a sign for **West Fork**, the trail made famous by Western novelist Zane Grey in *The Call of the Canyon.*

Fifteen miles into the trip you rise out of Oak Creek Canyon on tight switchbacks that take you up onto the Colorado Plateau. (A scenic overlook is available on top if you want a better look.) At about 25 miles or 45 minutes (longer if there is traffic), you'll turn right at the sign for I-17 (Flagstaff) and then left (north) off the overpass to enter the freeway. Within a couple of minutes, you'll exit on I-40 east, following the signs for Albuquerque. On I-40, watch for signs for Hwy 89A and the Grand Canyon. Exit up the ramp, turning left at the light onto another overpass, and turning right as you follow signs for Hwy 89A and Wupatki National Monument.

Hwy 89A takes you through the east side of Flagstaff, passing by the shopping mall and gradually turning north. As you leave the city limits, the speed limit increases. Watch for signs for **Sunset Crater Volcano National Monument** and **Wupatki Ruins**. The park road forms a semicircle that will eventually bring you back to Hwy 89, farther north. Consider buying a Golden Eagle pass here. The card, good for 12 months, will let you in any national park, including Grand Canyon, which will otherwise cost you $25 per vehicle.

I recommend stopping at the **visitor centers**, first at the crater and later at the ruins. A brief walk through the lava fields is enjoyable at Sunset Crater, as is a stop at the ruin sites in the Wupatki area. The volcano erupted nearly one thousand years ago. I like these stops because they give you a feeling of the geologic activity of the region that created the canyon, as well as a sense of the people that lived nearby.

181

Leaving the monument road, turn right onto Hwy 89A to head north. At the intersection with Hwy 64 at Cameron (see signs for Grand Canyon–South Rim), you have your chance to continue directly to the canyon. However, another interesting stop is just a mile further ahead. The historic **Cameron Trading Post** (past the bridge on the left) is a Navajo establishment that has the best shopping in the area. Food and gas are available here. Try the Navajo taco. The real treat, however, is to enter the private gallery, which most folks don't even realize is here. If you ask politely, the clerk will arrange for you to be escorted upstairs. This is where the real treasures are, including exquisite handmade rugs, pottery, and traditional Kachina dolls.

Turning onto Hwy 64, you'll travel to the less-crowded **East Rim** of the Grand Canyon. There is an interesting overlook along the way at the Little Colorado Scenic View, but by now you may be anxious to get to the canyon.

Stop at Desert View, the first overlook, and you'll see the **Desert View Watchtower**, built by architect Mary Jane Colter. Not far from here, Spaniards were the first Europeans to see the canyon in the 16th century. So poorly did they grasp the size of the canyon, they estimated the Colorado River to be only six feet wide.

The main advantage of this east-side approach is that you'll be able to travel at your own pace, stopping at whichever viewpoints you like. Meanwhile, the crowds on the tour buses from Phoenix and

Vegas are at Grand Canyon Village, forced to take the shuttle system around the west side. I recommend skipping the village, unless you want to stay overnight in style. In that case, the choice is **El Tovar**, with the best view of any lodge in the world. (Other options are lodges in the park, not on the rim, and a couple of hotels in the nearby town of Tusayan, about six miles outside the main entrance.)

182 A tiny fraction of the canyon's visitors set foot below the rim, so why not put yourself in this exclusive club? If **Bright Angel Trail** and **South Kaibab Trail**—the two best-known and maintained trails—are crowded, consider East Rim trails, which are equally scenic but less well known. Steep but beautiful are **Grandview Trail** (from the lookout of the same name) and **Tanner Trail** (which begins at Lipan Point). Remember, you're at a high altitude here, and you'll feel fine at first because you're going downhill. Stop before you get tired, not after, and allow twice the time for the hike back up.

You'd think that having seen the Grand Canyon **IMAX movie** 27 times now, I would be sick of it. No way. Located in Tusayan, along Hwy 64 just south of the canyon, the movie is worth a stop on your way back to Sedona. It plays at 30 minutes past the hour, every hour. Entertaining and educational, it will give you views from below to go with the ones you've had today from above.

The question is whether to stay for **sunset** (and drive home in the dark), or to head home in the daylight. The newspaper you'll be handed at the entrance gate will list the sunset time for that day as well as some nice places to watch it from. Coming home in the dark, the best route is Hwy 64 (south to Williams, not east to Cameron) to I-40 East. Off I-40, take the Phoenix/Sedona exit onto I-17, and then take the exit for Hwy 89A Sedona/Oak Creek Canyon. (If the switchbacks into Oak Creek Canyon really scare you, continue south on I-17 to Hwy 179 instead, for a longer but flatter alternative.)

Consider a compromise approach. Stay at Grand Canyon long enough for the beautiful late-afternoon light and shadows, so as to get the day's best photos. Leave before sunset though, and drive Hwy 64 south toward Williams (not east to Cameron), turning left onto Hwy 180 to Flagstaff. This route is just as fast but more scenic, passing the 12,000-foot high **San Francisco Peaks**, which may have snow on them. The glow on Kendrick Meadow and the tiny **Chapel of the Holy Dove** make a nice visual. There are aspen trees and ponderosa pine forests, as well as charred evidence of prior forest fires. Once back in Flagstaff, follow the signs for Phoenix and I-17 and take the exit for Hwy 89A Sedona/Oak Creek Canyon off the interstate.

The above route adds one to two hours to your trip on the way there, and remains a two-hour return ride.

183

OPTION 3
THE LONG WAY, BY TOUR VAN

If you'd like to take a tour to the canyon, **Great Ventures** is the low-cost mini-bus option. At $95 per person plus tax, the tour includes the Cameron Trading Post, lunch and the IMAX movie. **Pink Jeep Tours** offers a similar trip for slightly more. Each tour takes about 10 hours. Call Great Ventures at 800-578-2643 or Pink Jeep Tours at 800-873-3662.

OPTION 4
THE RAILROAD

The **Grand Canyon Railway** heads mostly through forest to get to the rim of the canyon. This trip is best for kids, seniors and people who are really into trains. The train delivers you to Grand Canyon Village, which offers a number of interesting buildings. If you'd like to see more views, consider arranging a tour so as not to feel stuck once you get off the train. The train departs Williams at 10am, arriving at Grand Canyon Village at 12:15pm. It departs Grand Canyon at 3:30pm, arriving to Williams at 5:45pm. Call 1-800-THE-TRAIN (843-8724) for reservations and directions. Class of service ranges from coach to "luxury observation," with adult tickets running from $54.95 to $139.95 and children's tickets from $24.95 to $109.95. At the canyon, tours range from 90 minutes to 2 hours, at $20 to $35 per adult.

OPTION 5
DRIVING THERE, FLYING OVER IT

If you'd like to drive to Grand Canyon and fly over it, then the choice is **Papillon Helicopter**, from $99 per person (928-638-2419, 800-528-2418) or **Air Star Airlines**, from $81 per person for 50 minutes (928-638-2139, 800-962-3869). They fly from Grand Canyon Airport, about six miles south of the main entrance.

184 ## OPTION 6
TAKE A VAN THERE, THEN FLY OVER IT

Papillon Helicopter also organizes a coach tour to Grand Canyon National Park combined with a 25-30 minute flight over the park. The tour includes viewpoints, with time to shop and walk along the canyon rim. Departs daily at approximately 9am and returns at 6:30pm. Adults $235; children (ages 2-11) $215. 928-638-2419, 800-528-2418.

OPTION 7
FLYING TO GRAND CANYON

For the full aerial excursion, you can fly to Grand Canyon Airport by plane or by helicopter from Sedona. There you'll transfer to a helicopter operator who will give you a 30-minute tour over Grand Canyon. The helicopter is faster and more costly. Its return trip includes views of Sedona's canyons and some high-placed ruins. The price is approximately $690 per person, including taxes and surcharges, with a two-person minimum. Reservations must be made at least several days in advance. Call **Arizona Helicopter Adventures**, 928-282-0904 or 800-282-5141. If you opt for the plane flight, $295 per adult, $225 per child, call **Sedona Sky Treks**. 928-282-6628, 800-578-2643.

OPTION 8
RAFTING THE COLORADO RIVER

Sedona Sky Treks offers another way to visit Grand Canyon, focusing on the Colorado River that made it all. You'll take a narrated bus tour north, skirting the Painted Desert to begin a river float just south of Lake Powell and Glen Canyon Dam. The tour touts "colorful rock formations, soaring wild life, ancient Indian petroglyphs, folklore and natural and human history." (It's a short hike to see the glyphs, by the way.) You'll come out of the river at historic Lee's Ferry. Lunch is included. Season: April 1 through October 15, Tuesday and Thursday. Departs from Sedona at 6:45am and returns at 6:45 pm. Adults $199, kids $169. 800-578-2643. To replace the bus legs with plane flights, you'll fly over the Grand Canyon and back to Sedona. Available March-October. 7 hours. Adults $365, kids $275. 928-282-6628, 800-578-2643.

OPTION 9

185

UP ABOVE AND OVER THE TOP

There is one last spectacular option. Tucked into the floor of the western Grand Canyon is the Havasupai Indian reservation, home of some of the world's most breathtaking waterfalls. **Sedona Sky Treks** offers to take you to the Grand Canyon South Rim airport by plane and transfer you to a helicopter for a 25-minute flight into the Grand Canyon. From there, it's an Indian-guided horseback ride to the base of the waterfalls. Heck, you can jump in if you like. You'll take a helicopter back out to Grand Canyon Airport, and fly back to Sedona on a plane. The entire trip is 10 hours. Adults $695, kids $545. Availability is limited, so call for details. 928-282-6628, 800-578-2643.

HIGHLIGHTS AT GRAND CANYON

Grand Canyon Village This complex of shops and lodges located on the South Rim is the best spot to hang out for those who are less mobile, but it also features the biggest crowds on weekends and every day in the summer. If time is an issue, then the Village need not be a mandatory stop. The views, although lovely there, are equally impressive elsewhere. Here are some of the Village's more interesting historic buildings.

El Tovar Known as "the" place to stay at the Grand Canyon, this wooden lodge is impressive. The lobby hosts gift shops, and there's an assortment of trophy heads in the Rendezvous Room. Watch as Japanese visitors shriek in delight (or is that terror?) at the javelina. Lunch, if you can get in, is the best meal around, but then again, there's not much around. Reservations are not accepted, which means you may have to decide on whether the wait is worth it. Reservations: 888-297-2757 or 303-297-2757. Switchboard: 928-638-2631.

Kolb Studio Built in 1904 on the edge of the rim is the former home of brothers Ellsworth and Emery Kolb, the first to film a Colorado River run through the canyon. Their black-and-white photography of a century ago is just as wonderful today.

Hopi House The work of architect Mary Jane Colter, Hopi House opened its doors next to El Tovar in 1904. Colter's vision, Hopi labor and native materials have recreated here the dwellings near Oraibi, considered by many archeologists to be the country's oldest inhabited town. In 1987 Hopi House was designated a National Historic Landmark, and in 1995, with Hopi consultation, the building was renovated. The trading gallery on the second floor offers museum-quality items. Summer: 8am-8pm. Winter: 9am-5pm. 928-638-2631, ext. 6383.

THE RIM DRIVES

Grand Canyon has a South Rim and a North Rim. The latter is over 200 miles further by car and closed each winter. If you're going for a day, you're going to the South Rim, which can be further divided into east and west sides. Free park shuttles run between the Village and Yavapai Point, Yaki Point, and Hermits Rest. The new visitor center complex is part information center and part shuttle bus depot. Here you'll find photography, charts, graphs, maps and displays exhibiting the wonders of the canyon.

West Rim Drive

The West Rim shuttle is required between March 13 and October 18, as West Rim Drive is closed to vehicular traffic during Grand Canyon's busiest season. The route includes Hopi, Maricopa, and Pima viewpoints and the 3,000-feet cliff wall known as the Abyss. Powell Point has a memorial to river runner John Wesley Powell and a view of Orphan Mine, one of the last used in the Grand Canyon. The road ends at Hermits Rest. There are bathrooms in this historic building designed by Mary Jane Colter, and you can buy snacks and gifts.

East Rim Drive

Generally, the East Rim Drive is less crowded, and although shuttle service is available, you can also travel it in your own car year-round. Note that East Rim Drive is 23 miles long, most of which will be at speeds of 30 miles per hour. This drive stretches between Mather

Point near the main entrance to Desert View at the east entrance. Stop at Yavapai Observation Station for an introduction to Grand Canyon geology.

Yaki Point offers glorious, unobstructed canyon views, best seen from the South Kaibab Trail, which leads into the inner canyon. The distinctive conical buttes that populate the canyon are clearly seen here. Shaped by the powerful erosional forces of wind and water, these stone monuments were dubbed "temples" in 1880 by geologist Clarence Dutton. Grandview Point was once host to Pete Berry's hotel and copper mines below, and the steep Grandview Trail begins here. Moran Point, named for painter Thomas Moran, also offers views of Hance Canyon, stomping grounds of the colorful John Hance, who also mined and took tourists into the canyon. Take a tour of Tusayan pueblo, a 12th-century Indian ruin, and its associated museum. Desert View is a splendid viewpoint, where the Vermilion Cliffs, San Francisco Peaks, Painted Desert and Colorado River come into view. It is the pièce de résistance of your drive. Climb Mary Jane Colter's Watchtower, and make use of the store, snack bar, restrooms, gas station (open seasonally) and gift shop.

187

TUSAYAN

The nearby township you'll pass through south of the main entrance holds the name of a place where Spaniards believed they would find treasures of gold. They never found gold or the legendary province, but you'll notice a few restaurants and hotels here. These accommodations provide a modern alternative to those within the park.
Grand Canyon IMAX View the movie *Grand Canyon: The Hidden Secrets*. Tickets are $10. The film shows on the half-hour throughout the day beginning at 9:30am. The last show is usually at 5:30pm. Highway 64, Tusayan. 928-638-2203.

TOURING OPTIONS

If you're heading to Phoenix instead of Sedona, then return on Hwy 64 south. Take Hwy 180 to Flagstaff, or stay on Hwy 64 to Williams and take I-40 east to Flagstaff. From Flagstaff, take I-17 south. If you're going to Las Vegas, take Hwy 64 heading south to Williams, then join I-40 West. Either destination is four hours away.

Flagstaff

PLANNING THE VISIT

The small city of Flagstaff offers dramatically different terrain, climate and geology from Sedona's, as well as some Native American treasures. At 6,900 feet above sea level, the air is clear, but the oxygen is thin. The impressive San Francisco Peaks are snow-capped most of the year, offering skiing in the winter and a cool retreat in the summer.

If you've never been to either Sedona or Flagstaff, it's worth considering the value of a high-country side trip. While you can't get to the Grand Canyon without going through Flagstaff, the truth is that a day at the canyon leaves you no time to explore this mountain town. I consider Flagstaff best as a cool getaway in the summer, a spot for aspen foliage in autumn, or a place to hit the ski slopes in winter. Still with so much to see, Flagstaff is a good option only if you've got more than four days in Sedona.

INTRODUCTION and HISTORY

Various tales about Flagstaff suggest that one of its tall Ponderosa pine trees was stripped and suited with a large American flag. Ever since, Flagstaff has been a station on the main line for trains, a rest stop on Route 66 for drivers and a gateway to the Grand Canyon for tourists. Arizonans love this mountain city for its cool temperatures. It is home to Northern Arizona University.

BUILDINGS and ATTRACTIONS

Museum of Northern Arizona This interesting museum holds particularly good collections in archaeology, geology, paleontolgy and art. Located three miles north of central Flagstaff on Hwy 180. 928-774-5213. www.musnaz.org

Walnut Canyon National Monument These thousand-year-old ruins are set in limestone walls in a forested canyon. Located seven miles east of Flagstaff. Take exit 204 on I-40. 928-526-3367.

Sunset Crater National Monument This is a crater volcano that erupted approximately a thousand years ago. Check out the Visitor Center, and then walk through the lava tubes and hardened basalt fields. From Flagstaff, take Hwy 89 north for 12 miles. Turn right at the sign for Sunset Crater Volcano/Wupatki National Monuments. The Visitor Center is two miles from this junction. 928-526-0502.

Wupatki National Monument Continuing on the road beyond Sunset Crater will eventually bring you to the outstanding ruins of Wupatki. With the snow-capped San Francisco Peaks behind them at a distance, these red-and-brown two-story residences were home to several different groups. The ruins are spread out, but accessible by paved roads. A renovated Visitor Center was recently inaugurated. The Visitor Center is 19 miles away from the Sunset Crater Visitor Center. 928-679-2365.

189

PLACES TO EAT and DRINK

Beaver Street Brewery You'll find tasty ales and very good food. 11 S. Beaver St., #1. 928-779-0079

Mogollon Brewery This popular spot offers colorful brews and colorful personalities in the heart of downtown. 15 N. Agassiz Street. 928-773-8950.

Macy's This coffeehouse, bakery and vegetarian restaurant is the beloved morning fill-up spot for students, professors, skiers and accidental tourists. 14 South Beaver Street. 928-774-2243.

Jackson's Grill For American cuisine, stop two miles south of Flagstaff on Hwy 89A. Look for it on the left-hand side as you are heading north, just past the llama ranch. 928-213-9332.

PLACES TO SHOP

Flagstaff's historic district downtown offers a variety of stores that reflect the interests of Flagstaff's eco-friendly, artistic and athletic locals. There are high concentrations of outdoor, camping, rock climbing and biking shops for such a small area, as well as off-beat stores offering Buddha statues, vinyl records and retro clothing. To get to this interesting district, follow I-17 as it enters Flagstaff, and stay on it until it becomes Route 66, approximately four miles, as it curves under the train tracks.

DRIVING TIME and DIRECTIONS

From West Sedona and Uptown, follow Hwy 89A north through Oak Creek Canyon. Fifteen miles ahead, you'll begin to wind up the hairpin curves that lead you to the Colorado Plateau. It is 28 miles to Flagstaff. An alternative route for those coming from the Village of Oak Creek is to head south on Hwy 179, then take I-17 north. Either way, the trip takes approximately 50 minutes. Snowy conditions can exist in the winter, and temperatures are 12 degrees cooler in Flagstaff than in Sedona during the day.

Northern Arizona's Great Places

With a healthy respect for the wonders of southern Arizona, the phrase of adventure around here is not "Go West," but "Go North." From Sedona northward exists natural beauty that stands as not just some of the country's best, but as some of the most amazing in the world. That's not all. Culturally, northern Arizona includes the reservation of America's largest native group and one of its most mythic tribes. Geologically, it holds clues to the ages of formation and erosion. Artistically, careers are made here, for those who capture the light through a lens or express it in a paintbrush.

Arizona's scenic beauty has been advertised, filmed and photographed for the viewing pleasure of people very far away. Don't feel foolish if you expect tall cactus in northern Arizona and instead find snow-capped mountains. Even many Arizonans are unaware of the state's diversity. I'm just pleased that you're interested and hope you'll find the time on this or a future trip to visit northern Arizona's most alluring places.

To help you feel a bit better informed on the region, here's a starter kit on special places north of Sedona.

ANTELOPE CANYON

The world's most photogenic slot canyon is best visited from the nearby city of Page, next to Lake Powell. During certain seasons angelic beams of light shine on orange sandstone ventricles that you can explore and photograph. Tours with Navajo guides are easy to find, and not expensive. Located due north, the driving time is three hours from Sedona to Page.

CANYON DE CHELLY

This narrow gorge in northeastern Arizona is home to ancient villages built by people who lived at the same time as Sedona's Sinagua people. Yet it is also home today to Navajos who continue to live in traditional hogans (a six-sided structure with a door facing east), farming and tending sheep. The Navajo word for the canyon is not Chelly, but Tsegi, and regardless of spelling is roughly pronounced "shay." The National Park Service offers a helpful visitor center, but as this is tribal territory only certain places are yours to explore without a Navajo guide. Lodging is available in the adjacent town of Chinle. Located north and east, the driving time is approximately three hours from Sedona.

HOPI MESAS

If portions of the Navajo reservation appear as if you've left the planet, then the Hopi Reservation or "Hopiland" will make you feel like you have gone back in time. Hopiland's oldest villages are atop three mesas, located right in the middle of the much larger Navajo reservation. Hopi prophecies have foretold that the tribe would always be economically poor, but spiritually very rich. So it is. The mesas are impoverished, but the traditions are rich and colorful. Although there's nothing to fear, the villages are not necessarily well-suited for visitation, and photography is often inappropriate or barred. The reward for your visit is an astonishing understanding of this fact: Within the U.S., there are many very different nations. Several routes lead north from Hwy 89A or I-40. It's a two- to three-hour drive, depending on the route.

THE PAINTED DESERT

The Painted Desert is really two places. To Arizonans, it is a large land mass, offering hundreds of miles of colorful terrain across northeastern Arizona and the Navajo reservation. It reveals soil only the designers at Crayola could have imagined—not just browns and reds, but black, white, green and purple. Considerable amounts of color can be seen traveling north toward Page or Kayenta on the Navajo reservation. To tourists looking for one spot to see it best, then Painted Desert is a stretch of colorful land conveniently located within Petrified Forest National Park, just off I-40. See below for directions to the national park.

PETRIFIED FOREST

Petrified Forest National Park is located south of I-40 and features the remains of an ancient forest that has been turned, literally, to stone. The crystalline logs are something to behold, gigantic cylinders of hardened color. To see the park, including the Painted Desert, head north to Flagstaff, then west on I-40 for about 80 miles. The trip takes a little over two hours by car.

LAKE POWELL

Imagine Sedona...with water. Okay, that's not exactly it, but it does give your brain something to consider. The Glen Canyon Dam (or Damn, depending on who you ask) turned a massive gorge of earth, ancient ruins and good river running into today's Lake Powell. Travel north to Flagstaff, west on I-40, then north on Hwy 89. It's about a three-hour drive.

METEOR CRATER

Over 4,000 feet across and 550 feet deep, this crater was formed millions of years ago. A remnant of the meteor remains for viewing. The crater once hosted America's astronauts when they were seeking training grounds for the moon. I-40, Ext 233, 35 miles east of Flagstaff. The trip takes a little more than an hour by car.

MONUMENT VALLEY

Home to mystical rocks, ridges and arches, Monument Valley has been the setting for dozens of films and hundreds of commercials. It is located on the Navajo Reservation on the Arizona-Utah border. You can drive in your own car for a fee, or you may choose a group tour or horseback riding adventure with Navajo guides. Bring lots of film, and try to time your visit for early or late in the day for best light. The Navajo town of Kayenta offers several nationally branded hotels in which to stay. Take I-40 west from Flagstaff, then north on Hwy 89A, then northeast on Hwy 160. It's about four hours from Sedona.

Northern Arizona Itineraries

Most of these sites require at least six hours of driving round trip, so make sure to gas up in Sedona.

— ONE DAY —

You can see the Petrified Forest National Monument, which includes Painted Desert. If there's time, you can view Meteor Crater on the return.

— ONE LONG DAY —

You can visit the Hopi Mesas, including the cultural center on Second Mesa.

— TWO DAYS —

You can get to Monument Valley and Canyon de Chelly, staying overnight in Chinle or Kayenta.

— TWO DAYS OR MORE —

You can visit Lake Powell and Antelope Canyon, staying overnight in Page or on a houseboat at the lake.

— THREE DAYS —

You could drive a large loop, visiting all the sites described above, except the Hopi Mesas.

— FOUR DAYS —

You could see all these places. Once you do, we can let you in on all the other, less well-known spots!

195

10

Answers to Frequently Asked Questions

Questions & Answers

Q: What is a vortex?

Sedona's most fascinating, controversial, delightful and confusing subject is its vortexes (or if you prefer, vortices). But while local experts are in abundance, visitors are often look confused and want to know what the heck is a vortex? For years, visitors have experienced strong feelings here that seem to be inspired by the beauty of the rocks, and yet not fully explained by it. From an increase in intuition to a sense of being at home, thousands report the phenomenon.

Although reports came far earlier, interest in this phenomenon peaked in the late 1970s and 1980s with the growth of the New Age movement in Sedona. Dick Sutphen led workshops on "psychic energy," and psychic and channel Page Bryant coined the word that gave the phenomenon the "brand" it required: vortex.

Commerce followed, with books, tours and the humorous vortex-in-a-can products among them.

What we know for certain is not always what you'll be told. You might be told that the iron in the rocks (which has colored them red) has created a magnetic field, and that this is the source of people's experiences. Further, many guides and stores will offer maps and tours to selected sites, as if this energy were sourced in individual spots.

Finally, after years of study, we know that the truth is different, although no less interesting. Geological study has demonstrated, on the one hand, that no such magnetism is present. The iron oxide has indeed impacted the rocks but merely as coloration. Likewise, to call certain spots magnetic, electric or electromagnetic (or masculine and feminine) is inaccurate. The "hard science" of measuring with traditional devices shows us no result.

On the other hand, after thousands of interviews and experiences, it is equally clear that people aren't "just making this up." Documented reactions suggest that those who are more sensitive to energy feel something here that makes Sedona more than such a pretty place. What are the reactions? They range from people moved spontaneously to emotion to feeling unusually healthy and vibrant to experiencing potent intuitions.

So why has the idea of magnetism stuck? For one thing, it is easy to grasp. For another, many visitors don't have time to explore the subject more deeply. Many locals don't understand it better, and others have a hard time explaining subtle energy.

A bit of advice. Consider a private tour but recognize that there are as many experts as there are Sedonans! If you choose to simply visit vortex spots and wait for it to "hit you," you'll see pretty places, but you may be disappointed. There is no correct spot to stand on and no correct way to feel it.

Instead, set your intention to have a deeper experience in Sedona, and recognize that no one visits by accident. Note who you see, what you see and how you feel, and know that all as it should be.

FOR FURTHER READING
What is a Vortex? A Practical Guide to Sedona's Vortex Sites
Having sold more than 25,000 copies, my own book has become the source for an understanding of Sedona's energy that is both practical and spiritual. It's available at most stores in Sedona, or on the web at www.MrSedona.com.

What makes the rocks red?

The iron minerals in the rocks have been altered and concentrated, giving the rock its red color. Iron oxide has, in effect, stained the rocks red, although there are no measurable concentrations of magnetism here. When more water and a thousand years or so are added to the red rocks, manganese forms. This appears as black stripes on the rocks where the summer rains flow. Locals call it Desert Varnish.

Q: What should I know about local wildlife?

Sedona's three-part terrain of high desert, riparian and mountainous zones shelters a variety of wildlife, and with a little extra effort, you can see some of it. Here's a primer.

We begin with mammals. If you see a dog running across Hwy 89A early in the morning, look again. It's probably not a dog but a **coyote**. Their coat is gray to gold to auburn in color, and they can be found individually or in packs. They are nature's ventriloquists; you're hearing just a few howling at the moon, not twenty! Far smaller is the **fox**, which comes in silver-colored varieties here. Seen a **javelina**? It looks a bit like a pig, a bit like a boar, and its English name is the collared peccary. These bristly critters have a snout and reddish eyes and weigh up to 50 pounds. Usually found in packs, they can't see for beans, but they sure can smell. Sedona has had a **desert cottontail** population explosion lately, but the big-eared, big-footed **jackrabbits** are the ones that will surprise you. Only at night can you see Arizona's state mascot, the **ringtail**. This creature is about two and a half feet long, but at least a foot of that is a black-and-white striped tail. **Mule deer** can blend motionless into the scenery or dash away in a high trot, leaping over brambles and cacti to slow their predators. Their name comes from their enormous ears. The **mountain lion** is king of cats around here. These are reclusive animals who typically stay away from local footpaths. You've got a slightly better chance to see a **bobcat**, a beautiful animal that's bigger than a housecat, with very big paws for its size. If you're looking for footprints, remember that cat tracks will not reveal claw marks, unlike those of canines. Speaking of paws, **black bears** are here in Sedona, but again, far from crowds. An exception is summertime, when they may seek food at campgrounds in Oak Creek Canyon. There are no grizzly bears in Sedona, and elk generally keep to the higher elevations.

As for reptiles, you'll see lots of lizards if you look down. A special treat is the **collared lizard**, which looks to be painted in brilliant green with silver-white and black stripes around its neck. The well-camouflaged **horned lizard**, popularly known as a "horned toad," looks like something out of the dinosaur era. If attacked, this reddish reptile can squirt blood out of its eyes. **Toads** can be heard mating in the late spring by water spots. As for snakes, first let me mention your odds of being bitten are less than that of being struck by lightning. Poisonous snakes do exist in the region, primarily rattlers, including the **mojave green** and **diamondback rattlesnake**. Since they are cold-blooded, they won't be out until the weather gets hot, and they avoid the high heat of summer midday.

201

Onto spiders and insects. As long as we're talking about critters that people get unnecessarily scared about, let's mention the **tarantula**. It's bite is not as bad as you've heard, and its black "fur" coat is more beautiful than you may realize. Look for males wandering roads and trails after an August rain storm. The unusual **desert centipede** is long and yet so quick that you may only see it for a second. Lots of legs—but not as many as a **millipede**. Mosquitoes are usually limited to creek areas. Ticks can be found in the forests to the north, but the Lyme disease of the eastern U.S. is not present. Rocky Mountain spotted fever, however, is a concern. You'll hate the "no-see-ums," aka **cedar gnats**. Avon Skin-So-Soft is said to repel them in the summer no-see-um season.

TIPS ON SEEING WILDLIFE
Go out when the animals are most active. When it is hot in the middle of the day, they'll be relaxing in hiding. Choose early morning or early evening instead, when many of Sedona's animals are moving about.

Keep quiet. Many animals can smell us long before they see us. Avoid perfumes and scented shampoos, which give your presence away. Be patient, and allow plenty of time. Appreciate those creatures that you do see. Don't take lizards for granted, just because they are more visible. Plants and trees grow vertically, so look for horizontal lines when scanning the wilderness to find animals. Look not for the deer, but for the deer's ear, which will lead you to the animal.

Do no harm to any creature you see. If it frightens you, just back away and leave. Remember, you're a visitor in their home. With the encroachment of development into their habitat, our animal populations are under stress and need all the care they can get. Finally, you've heard it before, but it's still true. Bring lots of water.

Just as much fun is tracking wildlife by looking for animal tracks and "scat," i.e. their droppings. Some sandy trails are a veritable anthology of wildlife stories—delicate quail tracks, the long line sketched by a lizard's tail, small cloven javelina prints leading to tasty plants. Going out after a rain or snow storm is an excellent opportunity to learn just how many critters we have by identifying their footprints.

WILDLIFE ATTRACTION
Out of Africa Wildlife Park

For views of more exotic animals, head to Camp Verde for this new park. You can walk the park or ride with a guide in a tour vehicle to see the giraffes, zebras, wildebeests and more. From the VOC, take I-17 South to Exit 287. Turn right onto Hwy 260, left onto Verde Valley Justice Center Road, then immediately right into the park. From UP, WS and OCC take Hwy 89A to Cottonwood. Turn left onto Hwy 260, then right onto Verde Valley Justice Center Road. Admission: Adults $28, kids (3-12) $20, seniors $26. Closed on July 4th, Thanksgiving and Christmas. Closed Mondays and Tuesdays, unless a major holiday falls on these days. Open Wed-Sun 9:30am-5:00pm (though admission closes at 4:00pm). www.outofafricapark.com

SIGNS and SYMBOLS

If you're interested in the symbolic meanings of the animals who cross your path in Sedona, check out *Medicine Cards*, by Jamie Sams. Available at **Crystal Magic**, **Crystal Castle**, **Sedona Crystal Vortex**, and other New Age stores or bookstores. Also helpful is the book *Animal Speak* by Ted Andrews.

Q: How can I take great photos in Sedona?

More people take more photographs in Sedona than in any place in Arizona except Grand Canyon. Yet when visitors get home, the pictures sometimes don't do this place justice. Here are some tips to ensure that your pictures will measure up. Happy shooting!

Shoot off-center. Our eyes are conditioned to expect things to be in the center. When you move things over, it draws the viewer's attention and interest. In addition, it allows you to show more of the background of your scene, a nice option in this beautiful terrain.

Shoot with the sun behind you. If this means sun in the eyes of your subjects, then count to three so that they can open their eyes for the photo. However, avoid blocking the sun and casting a shadow on your subject.

Fill your frame. See an object you want to shoot? Move or zoom in or out until you fill a substantial portion of the frame with it. At the same time realize that the sky itself, particularly deep blue sky with clouds, is also a subject worthy of inclusion.

Show scale. When shooting the big arch at Devil's Bridge, for example, have a friend stand nearby. That way people will really understand its size. Want to show how tiny a certain wildflower is? Photograph it with your finger next to it.

Shoot during "magic hour." In the hour after sunrise and the hour before sunset, nature's light takes on a vivid quality. Remember to shoot things that catch the sunlight, but don't photograph the sun itself. In Sedona, you'll notice that the red in the rocks picks up an orange glow during "magic hour," and the sky is a deeper blue. See the "Sunsets" chapter to understand specific times for your visit.

Stop standing around! Who needs another boring picture of two people standing up straight with their arms at their sides? Nobody. Instead, get your friends to freeze while they're bending, leaning, stretching, jumping, reaching or hugging. Posed, yes, but not looking posed.

Once you have the basics in mind, consider these advanced tips:

Tell a story. Take photos that will show the progression of your journey in Sedona. Shoot a sign that says "Sedona" on it, the name on the trailhead, or a calendar that shows the date. Along with the red rock scenery, show the car, jeep or helicopter that got you to the spot. Then, to go with your outdoor shots during the day, take some images to show what you were doing at night.

Focus on details. To balance your long-distance photos of the mountains, go in tight on small wildflowers, tiny rock images and little rivulets of water in the stream.

Think in themes. If your shots were to become a photo essay, what would you like the message to be? The options in Sedona are infinite: water on the creek, plays of light and shadow, sunrise and sunset, tourists having fun, celebration, contemplation.

Shoot with personality. How will your photos be different than anyone else's? What do your photos reflect about you and your style? Ask yourself these questions as you begin, and you'll find that you shoot more consciously. The results will express not just Sedona, but your unique view of it.

Shoot sideways. It's natural to take tall, vertical photos here. Make a point to take horizontal shots (called "landscape" format) of the red rocks, and you'll be surprised at the difference.

Appreciate the animals. Even if you can't find a bear to pose for you, there are colorful creatures everywhere you look. You may not see the eagle today, but don't miss the frog. Photographing animals in Sedona conveys a sense of the living wilderness in ways that pictures of rocks may not. To see coyotes, javelinas and the most colorful birds, get out there early…and stay late.

Keep only the best. Want a fast way to gain compliments for your photography? When you put together your collection after the trip, throw away any that aren't great! Instead of friends glazing over doubles of your average set of 36, they'll be wowed if you simply hand them your 10 best shots. And think of the storage space you'll save.

FILM DEVELOPING and DIGITAL PRINTING
Sedona Photo Express 150 Hwy 179, BTY. 928-282-6606
Walgreen's 1995 W Hwy 89A, WS. 928-282-2528.

CAMERAS and PHOTO EQUIPMENT
Rollie's Camera 297 N Hwy 89A, UP. 928-282-5721

Q: What's so special about Sedona sunsets?

Welcome to the place with sunsets so gorgeous that we put them on the flag. This is true for the State of Arizona, whose copper-colored star projects rays of red and gold light onto a base of blue sky. Likewise, Sedona's town flag displays the sun setting behind the fingered rocks of The Cockscomb formation.

Sunsets are important here. So here are a few things to know if you want to watch one, Sedona-style.

First, recognize that this is a region of beautiful sunsets. The metropolitan areas of Phoenix and Tucson further south can certainly stake their claim to great end-of-the-day beauty. Folks there look to the west, as you might expect, and watch as the setting sun casts the rays that inspired the state flag.

In Sedona, however, we do things differently. For one thing, there aren't usually many clouds around here most of the year. The lack of clouds means there is little for the sunlight to reflect off of in the sky above. Second, the presence of Mingus Mountain to the west blocks the sun anyway, meaning sunset comes a bit sooner than the tables would predict. In short, looking west doesn't usually offer much.

Ah, but there's so much to see in all the other directions! You see, during the "magic hour" or "golden hour" 30 to 40 minutes before and 10 to 20 minutes after the official sunset, Sedona is set aglow. Sandstone—essentially compacted silica—is tremendously reflective and catches the light.

So when the sun's final rays strike the red rocks, they pick up an orange glow, as if they were literally on fire. In the higher portions of the formations, the tannish-colored sandstone picks up a golden hue. The deep blues of the day sky are replaced by a background periwinkle. None of this happens in the western sky, where the sun itself is. That's how you can easily tell locals from tourists: They're looking in opposite directions!

Locals know that the most striking views are of formations with an eastern face. They also know that to figure out a formation's sunset potential, you need to understand the sun's movement through the sky during the year. Thunder Mountain (best seen from Airport Mesa) offers colorful views during winter and much of spring and autumn. Its southern face falls into shadow throughout summer, as the sun crosses higher in the sky and sets closer to due west.

206 With its broad views, Airport Mesa rarely disappoints, but other places are more reliable. One is the area between the Twin Buttes and Bell Rock. The buttes tower behind the Chapel of the Holy Cross, and paralleling Hwy 179 as it runs south are the impressive cliffs of Lee Mountain. Bell Rock, it is important to note, loses the sunlight at least an hour early, so arrive well ahead if you want photos of it. But even if Bell Rock is dark, you can see Courthouse Butte light up like a sparkler as it bathes in the warm sunlight. In fact, Bell Rock is perhaps the best place to watch the dusk entertainment in this area.

More famous is Cathedral Rock. This impressive formation asks you to make a choice to trust. Why? From down on the creek, you'll see hardly any of the sun at all. The trees of this riparian area block it, and the inexperienced will wonder if they've blown it, missing their chance for a pretty sunset. "What are we doing here?" they ask themselves.

And then it happens. Perhaps only by accident, they turn and look east to Cathedral Rock and bam! Sky rockets in flight! The rocks have been transmuted, tongues of flame into a blue sky.

Wishing doesn't hurt either. Am I exaggerating? I recall three occasions in which I wished for an extra-special sunset. On the first, a couple had hired me for a sunset tour on a cloudy summer day. With not a piece of sky in sight behind the clouds, I feared not enough sunlight would make it through. "There's a 98 percent chance that we'll get no sunset color at all folks," I said as I offered them the chance to reconsider our outing. But aware that all it takes is one good ray, I told them that we had a 2 percent chance of seeing the best sunset they had ever seen. They hesitated not a bit, strapped on their cameras, and followed me. Just over an hour later, I led them on a small visu-alization at a very scenic spot, as I often do with clients. When they opened their eyes, rays of sunlight touched Cathedral Rock as if painting it with gold dust and liquid fire. The gray rain clouds turned a violet purple as patches of periwinkle blue sky cleared.

My client looked at me between clicks of his camera and smiled. "Two percent," he said.

On another occasion, I ended an afternoon chat with a friend to meet some visitors up at Airport Mesa. I was not their hired guide that week but had become friendly with the group leader, and thought I would help them out. Before leaving my friend, I asked her to help me wish for a great sunset for these people. Upon arriving, I connected with the group, and took a stand upon a rock at the view point in order to be seen by the entire party.

I like to think of myself as an entertaining guide, but two minutes into my talk I noticed that nary an eye was laid upon me. They weren't just looking past me either: It was more like the look of the hypnotized. I knew that the moment had come. I turned and almost fell backwards off the rock. Dome-shaped Thunder Mountain had turned from warm afternoon light to a geological torch, and faint clouds above showed pink. When I next saw my friend, she complimented herself before I could: "Nice work, huh?"

The most amazing sunset of all came early in my guiding career, when a television crew appeared with questions for a story. As the day ended, we made another of those wishes.

What happened next was remarkable. To the east, Snoopy Rock and the Schnebly Hill formations picked up the orange colors that we expect. What wasn't planned was the massive moon, nearly full, on the rise. To the north the colors on Thunder Mountain and Coffee Pot were even more gorgeous. Most surprising of all, the western horizon provided something I had never seen. Clouds in the sky picked up pink and lavender all around, while beneath them genuine lightning bolts struck in the distance. It was if the heavens had parceled enough clear sky to see the sunset, and enough clouds above it to offer color. Bridging the two, the fingers of lightning seemed like cosmic visual effects.

Have I made too much of the sunsets? On some days, certainly so. But we live for the others.

PLACES TO WATCH A SUNSET

Airport Mesa Drive 1.1 miles west of the "Y" and turn left up Airport Road. The dirt pullout is fine for views, but most people continue to the lot on top of the mesa. Cross the street carefully to the overlook.

(208) **Red Rock Crossing** Head west on Hwy 89A, approximately four miles from the center of Sedona. Turn left at the stoplight onto Upper Red Rock Loop Road. As the road begins its winding descent, you'll see a number of left-hand pullouts for picture taking. Take a left turn onto Chavez Ranch Road. Follow the winding paved road to Crescent Moon Ranch Park entrance on the left. It's a few dollars to enter, and your Red Rock Pass does not cover the entrance fee.

Twin Buttes–Bell Rock Area Drive south on Hwy 179, four to six miles below the "Y." Note that shadows will cover Bell Rock an hour before the rest of the formations. I recommend arriving early to see the colors on Bell, and then walking to its eastern side. There you can sit and watch the show on Courthouse Butte and the ridges beyond it.

Of course, there are many more sunset hotspots. I'll leave you the pleasure of finding them yourself!

SEDONA SUNRISE/SUNSET
Mountain Standard Time

	MONTH	SUNRISE	SUNSET		MONTH	SUNRISE	SUNSET
1	Jan	7:35am	5:27pm	1	Jul	5:17am	7:45pm
15		7:34am	5:39pm	15		5:25am	7:41pm
1	Feb	7:26am	5:56pm	1	Aug	5:37am	7:30pm
15		7:13am	6:10pm	15		5:47am	7:16pm
1	Mar	6:57am	6:23pm	1	Sep	6:00am	6:54p
15		6:38am	6:35pm	15		6:10am	6:34pm
1	Apr	6:14am	6:48pm	1	Oct	6:22am	6:11pm
15		5:56am	6:59pm	15		6:33am	5:53pm
1	May	5:37am	7:12pm	1	Nov	6:48am	5:33pm
15		5:24am	7:23pm	15		7:01am	5:22pm
1	Jun	5:15am	7:35pm	1	Dec	7:16am	5:16pm
15		5:13am	7:42pm	15		7:27am	5:17pm

Q: What can you tell me about Sedona real estate?

If you find yourself with a wonderful case of Red Rock Fever, there is only one known cure: to stay. Here are a few points to consider if you are interested in buying a home or property in Red Rock Country.

The Price: The median home price in Sedona passed the half-million dollar mark in 2005 and continues upward. Stunned? So are Sedonans.

The Locations: Sedona's west side is our most residential area. Once you're beyond the tourist strip, Uptown is surprisingly quiet and offers lovely residential opportunities that are often overlooked. The Village of Oak Creek was once the less expensive side of town, but that won't be true much longer. The presence of two beautiful golf courses, improved dining options and upscale housing means the Village is moving on up.

The Seasons: If you like sunshine, you'll like Sedona. However, Sedona does have more than one season. It can snow in winter and get hot in the summer. Make sure to work with someone who knows the area to anticipate the impact of summer heat, thunderstorms, and winter cold on your potential purchase.

The Routes: Avoid tunnel vision. It is easy to focus only on well-trafficked streets around highways 89A and 179. However, if you spend some time examining the nooks and crannies of interior neighborhoods, you'll see land and homes that miss the spotlight.

The Papers: If you're thinking of moving here in the future, consider a subscription to the bi-weekly *Red Rock News* (928-282-6888), the monthly *Red Rock Review* (928-282-0008), *Sedona Monthly* 928-282-1855) or the quarterly *Sedona Magazine* (928-282-9022). These periodicals can keep you up to date on the issues around here.

The Demography: Statistics say that Sedona is the most economically segregated city in Arizona. Increasingly, this is a town of the rich and the poor. Most of the former brought their money with them; the latter earn theirs with wage jobs in the tourism industry. Like other Arizona towns, Sedona has nearly doubled in population in a little over a decade. The pressure to grow will continue, but most of the greenery left is National Forest. This means prices for available private land are likely to go higher.

210

The Sticker Shock: If you're overwhelmed by Sedona real estate prices, know that your dollar goes much, much farther in neighboring communities. Cottonwood, Camp Verde, Cornville, Rimrock and Lake Montezuma are dramatically less expensive. The drawback is that you're beyond the red rocks. Living in these towns, you'll consider Sedona akin to being in a city with opera: You may not go daily, but it's nice to know that whenever you want to, you can.

REAL ESTATE AGENT

Dennis Andres is a licensed Re/MAX agent. Clients choose "Mr. Sedona" as someone who understands Sedona's past, but more importantly, knows where it is going. Call his office at 928-204-2201 if you're interested in learning more.

SENIOR LIVING

Sedona Winds This is a senior facility offering several levels of service. To check it out, turn east at the stoplight by the outlet mall in the Village of Oak Creek, and follow less than a mile on Jacks Canyon Road. 475 Jacks Canyon Road, VOC. (928) 284-9077

Q: What is the ancient history of Sedona?

FIRST PEOPLES

Thanks to evidence such as ancient human etchings on the red rocks, we know that native people resided here more than 5,000 years ago. Our understanding of these peoples is limited, but it seems that they survived by gathering nuts and berries in the forests, as well as hunting wild game. Though it took effort, there was enough of each: acorns, prickly pears and pine nuts to collect; quail, rabbits and deer to track.

In harmony with that lifestyle, it would be natural to move with the seasons. Sedona's winter temperatures are generally moderate and the rim country offers cool weather in the summer. So it seems that long before Arizona ever got Sun City, it had snowbirds, as these ancient peoples moved between the red rocks and the Colorado Plateau.

GETTING THE NAMES STRAIGHT

You may have heard the word "Anasazi" thrown around, but here are three good reasons not to get attached to it. First, the professor that picked it was looking for a Navajo word for "ancestor." He goofed. More properly translated, it means "ancient enemies." Second, these were not ancestors of the Navajo anyway, and the Navajo themselves came from elsewhere. Third, there is another group of people to whom the term is more commonly applied. The Anasazi are associated with the ruins of Mesa Verde (in Colorado) and Bandelier (in New Mexico), as well as other sites.

Lacking a better name, many here have simply chosen to call prehistoric people the Ancient Ones.

A CHANGE OF PACE

Blissfully ignorant of the future nomenclature issues their very existence would create, these ancient peoples practiced this hunter-gatherer lifestyle not for decades or centuries, but for millennia. It was almost 2,000 years ago when a significant change would alter their relation to the land: They adopted farming. This very small-scale agriculture included corn, squash and later, beans. Tending fields required something different: settling down in one place all year long.

Around the year A.D. 650 a new civilization emerged in an area from the San Francisco Peaks south through the Verde Valley that surrounds present day Sedona. Known as the Sinagua, they prospered in the area for seven centuries and built many pueblos. By then, the Ancient Ones were as ancient to the Sinagua as the Sinagua are to us. The name itself comes from the Spanish words "sin" (without) and "agua" (water), a reference to the San Francisco Peaks, dubbed by Spanish explorers as "the mountain without water," or the Sierra sin Agua de San Francisco.

212

SINAGUA LIFE

As is typical of modern humans, we underestimated the knowledge and technology of our predecessors by presuming that the Sinagua had little contact with other ethnic groups of the region. Not so. They participated in trade routes that stretched for great distances in the four directions. Traders dealt in cotton and clothing textiles, turquoise and precious stones, seashells used as coin and fashion items. Most impressive of all, routes extended south all the way into Mexico and Central America. The exotic feathers of macaws were brought from there, perhaps useful in the ceremonies of the Sinagua.

Dwellings of the Sinagua are found across the Verde Valley today. Sites include Tuzigoot, where three large pueblos sit on a ridge above the banks of the Verde River. West of Sedona are Palatki and Honanki, which feature dwellings nestled under impressive red rock cliffs. You can see ancient petroglyphs and pictographs here too. South of Sedona is the site known as Montezuma Castle, where a five-story, 20-room dwelling and a six-story, 45-room dwelling rest magnificently in white-gray limestone walls above Beaver Creek. This area also shows influences from the Hohokam, who lived primarily in the areas around modern-day Phoenix.

MOVIN' ON

The more one studies the history of the Southwest, the more one realizes that migration isn't just an important part of the story: It is *the* story. As ancient ones before them and modern Arizonans after them, the Sinagua migrated. In the middle of the 14th century, they moved away from their pueblos. Why they went remains controversial, but drought was one possible cause. We now know that a two-decades-long period of reduced rainfall occurred that same time.

213

More recent evidence comes from another nearby site of importance, Montezuma Well. This natural spring was a source of water for the Sinagua, which they channeled as irrigation for their fields. Historians believe that the Sinagua left 20 years after irrigation from the Montezuma Well peaked. Richard D. Foust, Jr., Professor of Chemistry at Northern Arizona University, has demonstrated that the well has high amounts of arsenic, nearly 20 times higher than recommended levels. Bones of animals that would have also been part of the Sinaguan's diet have been shown to have arsenic levels 100 times higher than normal.

OTHER CULTURES

Migration was not nearly finished. From the north came the Apache and Navajo. From the south came the Yavapai, originating from Yuman-speaking peoples known as the Pai. Yavapai means "People of the Sun," and members of this tribe hunted and gathered in the region as early as 1300. In 1875, the cavalry marched hundreds of Yavapai people east to the San Carlos Reservation, where they lived and intermarried with the Tonto Apache. In the early 1900s their descendants were allowed to return to the Verde Valley. Many became farmers at the encouragement of the U.S. government, settling near the army's Fort Verde, in the heart of present-day Camp Verde near Sedona. The Yavapai-Apache have been one formal nation since 1934, and their reservation rests around Camp Verde and Clarkdale.

MORE ON SEDONA'S ANCIENT HISTORY

For details on Palatki, Honanki, V-Bar-V, Tuzigoot, Montezuma Well and Montezuma Castle, see "Indian Ruins" in the Outdoors chapter.

Q: How can we have a great family vacation?

With Sedona's more mature population, it can be tough to find kids here, whether as locals or visitors. So to make your family's vacation great will require a lot of extra information. This should help.

It's amazing that the list of family-friendly **accommodations** is far smaller than the list of pet-friendly ones! Properties that welcome families include Quail Ridge Lodge (VOC, 928-284-9327. www.quailridgeresort.com), and the Radisson Poco Diablo (BTY, 800-333-3333) is located off Hwy 179. Los Abrigados (800-521-3131), just south of the "Y" and offers a great list of activities and amenities, including miniature golf. All three offer some combination of rooms, food or amenities that make them good family choices. A young family I know from Phoenix loves to head up Oak Creek Canyon to Junipine Resort (928-282-3375). There's room for their two kids and grandma all in one large creekhouse, and the food is delicious at the café. For a more upscale stay, the casitas at Enchantment Resort (928-282-2900, 800-826-4180) are a surprisingly good option for families. Camp Coyote will help provide things to do for the children.

Young people have energy. What **activities** are here for them? This is a great chance to introduce them to nature. Of course, Sedona has dozens of trails to choose from, but avoid trails with steep drop-offs, such as Devil's Bridge. Carruth Trail is a far gentler **nature trail** (see Walking) and even has the names of many plants written on signage below. Sedona Sports (251 Hwy 179, BTY, 928-282-1317) offers baby backpacks if you need some help to carry your little one.

If your kids demand a little more excitement, let them be **cowboys (or cowgirls)** for a day at M Diamond Ranch (30 minutes south of Sedona, 928-300-6466). In addition to a horseback ride, they'll learn more about how a genuine working ranch operates. For more cowboy flavor, visit the Blazin' M (928-634-0334), a working ranch that offers a Western theatre show at night. If you need more exotic creatures to entertain your children, then Out of Africa Wildlife

Park is a must, with giraffes, zebras and more. See them as you walk, or from aboard a guided safari vehicle (www.outofafricapark.com).

Except for very small children, most kids squeal with delight on **jeep tours**. In fact, it's a wonder they let adults on at all. Try Red Rock Jeeps (928-282-6826, 800-848-7728) on their adventure through Soldiers Pass. Devil's Kitchen and the Seven Sacred Pools can be seen on this ride. If you want to try a jeep ride, horseback ride and cookout, contact A Day in The West (928-282-4320). Part of your adventure will be to head through an authentic movie set used for filming Westerns.

215

If you'd like to get your kids into the **fishing** tradition with ease, check out Rainbow Trout Farm (3500 N Hwy 89A, OCC, 928-282-5799) and have a meal while you're at it! "Everything you will need to hook 'em and cook 'em." The fish are raised in artesian springs, and the farm features grills and picnic tables in a green setting. No license is required, and the farm is open daily.

Teenagers have their own tastes, of course, and although they'd enjoy the horses and jeeps they may have even more fun on a **mountain bike**. It's a feeling of freedom and adventure that teens love. Bike & Bean (6020 Hwy 179, VOC, 928-284-0210) and Absolute Bikes (6101 Hwy 179, VOC, 928-284-1242) are located close to the Bell Rock Pathway, which is a great route for beginners. Sedona Sports has nice starter deals too. For teens who want to feel the power of an engine, how about an all-terrain vehicle adventure? Arizona ATV Adventures is ready to ride (1185 W Hwy 89A, WS. 800-242-6335). If it's raining outside, there's **bowling** at Shake, Rattle and Bowl (Cliff Castle Casino, exit 289 off I-17, 928-567-7950).

When you're ready to **eat out**, there's Red Planet Diner (W Hwy 89A, WS) for fun. The Hideaway (251 Hwy 179, BTY, 928-282-4204) is a value-oriented Italian restaurant, and Wildflower Bread Company (Piñon Pointe, 101 N Hwy 89A) is clean and easy, adding pasta dishes in the evening to the sandwiches and soups they serve all day. The Cowboy Club (241 Hwy 89A, 928-282-4200) has a Southwestern approach, and there's always something that tickles kids, from cactus fries (made from the prickly pear cactus) to rattlesnake to ostrich.

Q: How can I create my own personal retreat?

What is so special about Sedona that it allows people to make positive shifts in their life while here? Why are even short visits so memorable? Maybe it's the weather, with sunny days year round. Perhaps it is the spectacular scenery that lifts one's spirits. Maybe it's the clean air, which seems to breathe new life into people. Don't forget the gentle places to walk, and the lovely, flowing creek. Perhaps there really is a unique energy here that turns your intentions into reality.

The statistics show that most of Sedona's tourists (now numbering in the millions) pass through the town, rather than get to know it. Increasingly, however, more of those millions are choosing to stay longer. If you are seeking a place to make changes in your life, Sedona is it. Here I have seen people process the grief of losing loved ones, give up the struggle of bad relationships, release old patterns, and launch new dreams.

There are lots of organized retreats and personal growth workshops offered each year, but if you're looking for something to do by yourself, here are a few pointers.

Set your intention. Before you begin, decide what you'd like to focus on during your personal retreat. Is it a health concern that needs attention? Maybe it's a relationship to be ended, or to be created. Is it your career that demands re-thinking? Being clear with your intention will begin to attract the people, places, and situations that help create what you desire. If you didn't get to it sooner, the two-hour drive from the airport is the perfect opportunity for intention-setting.

Find accommodations first. With a base to start at, you can unpack and relax. This will provide your anchor while you go out and explore. The number one thing that people fail to do to ensure lodging happiness is simply to check the room itself. If you're making reservations before you come here, get on the web to preview the room. If you're already here, simply ask to see it. You'll want someplace quiet, preferably with a small fridge.

Buy a journal and write each day. What should you write about? Whatever comes to mind. In fact, write exactly what comes to your mind, and see where it goes. At some point during the day, make sure to write down what things in your life you'd like to release or bring to a close. On a different occasion, list some of the new dreams you'd like to imagine for yourself.

Spend time in the world's greatest healing chamber: nature. Like our own bodies, nature is a complex system composed of organisms living and working in harmony. When your system is out of balance, placing it in the middle of nature's equilibrium seems to encourage gentle, healthy shifts. In particular, take note of the elements. Spend some time in a place with a gentle breeze or strong wind. Allow yourself to soak up some sunshine. Walk the red earth, and sit upon the stones. Finally, find your way to Oak Creek and listen to its gentle flow.

Listen to some music. It really does work to set the mood. So bring a Walkman or I-Pod for your walks and a tape player for the room. You'll find soothing music on sale available throughout town, some of it recorded by local musicians whose songs are just right.

Let someone else take care of you. Sedona is one of the country's foremost sites for alternative healers, massage therapists, and counselors. From individuals to healing centers to treatment institutions, the town is packed with the resources you'll need to create change in your life. Take advantage of them. Likewise look for the town's health food stores. Just as eating poorly can suppress emotions, eating healthfully can be an enormous help in releasing them.

Visit Sedona's special places. Among them should certainly be the Chapel of the Holy Cross, the architectural vision of a woman who dreamed of a place that would express a more modern spirituality. Go to the places you feel drawn to. This may mean visiting a place with a name that has meaning for you or tracking down a place you've seen in a picture. While the town is famous for specific vortex locations, realize that the energy here is actually all around. Going into red rock country, you simply can't go wrong.

Follow these seven steps with commitment, and you'll leave Sedona on the path to your dreams.

PERSONAL GROWTH RESOURCES

If you'd like to join a retreat someone else is setting up, here are some places to start your search. Sedona-based events tend to fall into the category of personal growth and alternative healing.

218

Barbara Marciniak is a gifted channel who comes to Sedona in March of each year. She speaks at 7 Centers Yoga Arts. 2115 Mountain Rd, WS. 928-203-4400. www.7centers.com

Meditation Coach Sarah McLean has impeccable credentials and offers private sessions that clients find very helpful. She is an excellent life coach too. 928-204-0067. meditate@esedona.net

Myofascial Release Founder John Barnes returns to Sedona each year to teach his innovative healing method at Therapy on the Rocks. 676 N Hwy 89A, UP. 928-282-3002.

The Sedona Creative Life Center offers lots of events during the year. Recent highlights have been medical intuitive Dr. Judith Orloff and creativity and writing experts Natalie Goldberg and Julia Cameron. 928-282-9300. www.sedonacreativelife.com

The Sedona Method Founder Hale Dwoskin teaches this emotional release method around the world, but here too. 928- 282-3522, 888-282-5656. www.sedona.com

A Woman's Way Karen Ely's retreat program is a great resource for women interested in personal growth. www.awomansway.com

Q: How can we have a romantic Sedona weekend?

Lots of visitors choose Sedona to create or reignite *l'amour* in their lives. They've picked the right place. There's something about Sedona that seems to make falling in love very easy. Here are some suggestions to make your visit more romantic.

Let's begin with **amenities**. Flowers can be purchased at Sedona Floral on the west side. Exceptional chocolate truffles are available at the west-side Ravenheart coffee hangout and more exotic candies at Sedona Fudge Company in Uptown. You can find the perfect bottle of champagne at Top Shelf Liquor on the west side or at Sedona Liquors below the "Y." Check Art of Wine in Uptown or the Wine Basket at Hillside if it's the ideal red wine you seek. If you'd rather rely on professionals to handle the job, call on Gift Baskets of Sedona to put it all in the perfect package. Looking to ride in style? White Tie or Luxury Limousines may have something for you.

Next, let's look at **romantic accommodations**. This is where Sedona's B&Bs, cabins and small inns really excel. Cozy and friendly, they let you be private when you want to be and sociable when you choose. The Inn on Oak Creek and the Wishing Well are best among B&Bs for romantic ambience. The former overlooks the creek, and rumors are the Duck Pond room gets the most "activity" among lovers. At the Wishing Well, you can stay in bed and have breakfast brought into your room, or soak in a hot tub under the stars at night. For a high country feeling, the Canyon Wren cabins are located up Oak Creek Canyon, which makes them best in warmer months, unless you like snow. Slide Rock State Park is nearby.

Then there are **romantic activities**. If your loved one doesn't mind a very early start, then he or she can't fail to be impressed by a hot air balloon ride, complete with champagne breakfast. If you're here on a weekday, stroll through Uptown if you'd like to do some shopping, and have lunch on the balcony of Canyon Breeze. On the weekend, try Tlaquepaque instead. It's nice for window-shopping, with pleasant arches, porticos and fountains to enjoy with your sweetheart. You can take a peek at the small chapel here, and have lunch at the Secret Garden Café.

If romance means the **outdoors** to you, then Oak Creek Canyon is a must. For a hike, try West Fork, which inspired the romantic novel *The Call of the Canyon* by western writer Zane Grey. Or, for a shorter walk, try Slide Rock State Park. Even gentler—and closer to the heart of town—is Grasshopper Point, also on 89A. At any one of these sites, the creek flows musically. If you want to be by the water without all the exercise, have lunch and be served in style by the creek at L'Auberge de Sedona.

If you like **romantic sunsets** but just can't wait that long, something interesting happens over at Enchantment Resort. The tall canyon walls pick up the sun's glow hours before the actual sunset. Make reservations for Tii Gavo Grill and get a seat on the deck for a lovely view. When true sunset arrives, where should you be? Take your rental car up Schnebly Hill Road. If it's your own car or it doesn't have high clearance, proceed just half a mile past the pavement. Here the road widens and you can park by the big boulders. If you've got more time and a 4WD, it's a bumpy 15-minute ride a few miles up to Merry-Go-Round rock. Pull over and enjoy spectacular views. Linger with your loved one just a bit after the sun is down. If there any clouds in the sky, this is when they will catch the best color. Be careful of the edge of the road on the dark ride down.

Another option is Crescent Moon Ranch, home of a romantic sunset story. It seems a couple came from the Midwest, saw the sunset here...and now live in Sedona, tending to the park. Stroll by the creek here at **Red Rock Crossing** and watch the setting light on Cathedral Rock.

If you're looking for dinner to clinch the deal, then you're in luck— **romantic dining** is a specialty in Sedona. Take it from a bachelor who has been around town: When the night really matters, head to René of Tlaquepaque. A booth is best for privacy, and nothing works for tingles like their very tall glass of champagne. The chocolate soufflé desert must be pre-ordered, so mention it when you call for reservations. Later, you can stroll through Tlaquepaque. Alternatively, choose the Gallery on Oak Creek at Amara Resort and sit near the fire pit. Nice touch. It's all about *amore* at Cuccina Rustica, and the entire restaurant seems made to dazzle you and your date. If romance means animal passions, and animal passions mean meat-eating, then Savannah restaurant is best for steaks.

Not ready to head back to the room? Steak & Sticks is open late for cocktails and billiards. Alternatively, fluteplayer Jesse Kalu provides music that is just native–New Agey enough to put you into a romantic mood. Look for his one-hour evening performances in town on weekends. Or make your own entertainment at Airport Mesa. The crowds are there at sunset, but at night, the town glistens below you. Walk out to the observation area, but be careful of the barrier: There's no light up here to see by. Look left toward the west and see what a buddy of mine calls Constellation Jerome. The old mining town perched on the side of Mingus Mountain appears to be a set of stars in the sky.

FIVE ROMANTIC DINNER TABLES

When it has to be right, here's where to sit.

1. Savannah's. While Table 25 works in general, only one place will do for a really big night: the cabin. Located on the property but away from the main restaurant, it offers completely private dining by a fireplace ($500 includes a custom-designed meal).

2. Cuccina Rustica has an entire romance room complete with "stars" above. Ask for Table 36.

3. Gallery on Oak Creek, Amara Resort offers outdoor seating. Table 81 is by the fire pit.

4. René. Best bets—the booths to the left are the most intimate.

5. Dahl & DiLuca is lively at night. Try Table 15 for increased coziness.

TOP 10 MAKE-OUT SPOTS

Now really, is any other guide book offering this? Here are a few recommendations for kissing, day and night. Feedback welcome.

DAYTIME

1. Airport Mesa vortex. Turn north off W Hwy 89A onto Airport Road and pull over to the dirt parking lot on the left. Climb the hill and tell your partner you've got just the method to feel the energy!

2. Red Rock Crossing. This is more than just a spot to kiss. This is a spot to propose. The center right formation of Cathedral Rock is known as Lovers Rock.

3. Courthouse Butte Loop. On a long afternoon walk, this trail provides a number of nobody-will-see-us-here spots.

4. Chapel of the Holy Cross. Too holy for more than a peck, but kisses here at the chapel's front plaza have the air of the sacred about them. (They also have an air of commitment, so proceed carefully.)

5. Sugarloaf. Near famous Coffee Pot Rock is a scenic, smaller hill called Sugarloaf. Find your way to this neighborhood trail and take the hearty 20 minute hike up. Kiss to a 360-degree view.

Bonus Skinny-Dipping Spot: Head for Oak Creek below Midgley Bridge. Park at the bridge and hike down the winding trail. Cross the footbridge and meander on the path, looking left for the main creek. Beyond the large boulder, there's a deep spot in the otherwise shallow stream.

Bonus Low-Impact Exclusive Make-Out Spot: If you or your date is a guest at Enchantment Resort; the property has a spire just above called Kissing Rock. Make good use of it. If you aren't guests, best to kiss and admire it from afar.

NIGHT TIME

1. Tlaquepaque. The Patio del Norte courtyard has a nice fountain. You can take the staircase to the open area above. If shopping is therapy, then kissing here makes medical sense.

2. Hillside Galleries fountain. Between the wine shop and Javelina Cantina, you can sit and listen to the frogs at night. If there's too much noise, move to the back staircase. Another choice is the upper level. There's a central water feature here and benches offering relative privacy at night.

3. Airport Mesa Overlook. Drive up Airport Road to the top of the mesa, turning left into the gravel parking lot. Park and walk back across the road to the paved overlook to see the town glittering below.

4. Bell Rock at full moon. The path is visible during bright moonlight for an extra-terrestrial smooch.

5. Schnebly Hill. For those that like a kiss in the style of an old-time drive-in theater, take the very bumpy road just far enough to see the town lights at a distance.

CONTACT NUMBERS

Sedona Limousines 928-204-1383.
Gift Baskets of Sedona 2160 Shelby Drive, WS. 928-282-7747.
Sedona Floral 928-282-3448.

Q: How can we save money in Sedona?

In the low-priced State of Arizona, you've entered an island of price inflation. It takes a special effort and some inside information to find ways to save money around here. The good news is that Sedona's best asset—**the view**—is free!

Your least expensive sleep options got a little costlier when the Forest Service began limiting where you can **pitch a tent** outdoors. You can backpack a couple of miles into the forest, but car camping is restricted to official campsites throughout Oak Creek Canyon. The cost is $15 per night. (See "Camping" for details.)

If you can't part with your **pets**, or can afford a little more, then try the White House Inn, which is usually among the least expensive spots along Hwy 89A on the west side.

There are great bargains to be had around town in the **winter off-season**, which begins after Thanksgiving weekend. Exceptions would be the Christmas–New Year's week, and the weekend closest to Valentine's Day. Summer, our other off-season, also features lower rates from the moderate Kokopelli Suites to the upscale Enchantment Resort. Many B&Bs offer three-night stays for the price of two.

Most **coffeehouses** have some rule against taking three hours to drink your one cup of coffee. Buy it at Ravenheart in Uptown, however, and you can go outside and watch the tourists and the mountains all day long. **Bagels** are a cheap way to fill up: Try New York Bagels. For a bigger **breakfast**, Café Jose in the Safeway Plaza is economical.

For **lunch**, begin by plunking down 50 cents for the Friday edition of the *Red Rock News*, or just check around for a free copy of *The Scene*, the paper's weekend section. Here you'll find **coupons** for India Palace and other local restaurants. While the **sandwiches** are not particularly cheap at Sedona Memories, they're big enough to cover lunch and dinner. Call in advance and get a free cookie with your order! Delicious choices come meaty or vegetarian at EuroDeli, with many sandwiches priced under $5.

For **dinner**, the Hideaway serves good, reasonably priced Italian food, even less expensive with their 20 percent VIP card. You can pick one up at the Chamber of Commerce. While there, check out the Chamber's Sedona Superpass **coupon book** for discounts all around town. If your small budget and big appetite come into conflict, you won't go hungry at Joey Bistro at Los Abrigados. Several mid-week nights feature **all-you-can-eat** deals.

225

The good news is that the **hiking** is still free, although the Forest Service may ask you to pay for the parking. (See "Parks and Passes" for details.) As for sites, absolutely free is the beautiful Chapel of the Holy Cross, located on Chapel Road, off Hwy 179 north of Bell Rock. (It's free of charge, not free of tourists.) From here you'll see Bell Rock, Cathedral Rock, Courthouse Butte and Lee Mountain. To get the views that the tour companies offer, visit Airport Mesa on the west side of town. To be by the **creek** without paying for it, stop at Indian Gardens in Oak Creek Canyon. Or, drive north past Slide Rock State Park, squeeze into a safe parking spot on the left side of 89A, and shimmy down to the water for free. The rangers don't mind, but be careful to stay off the narrow road.

What about inexpensive **entertainment**? Most fine dining establishments have musicians playing background music as you dine. For a real show, cover charges in Sedona are cheap compared to cities elsewhere. Shows at Relics, Casa Rincon, Olde Sedona and Full Moon Saloon range from free to $10. Entertainment at The Oak Creek Brewery on the west side is almost always free and sociable. Meanwhile, soulful fluteplayer Jesse Kalu plays on Saturday and Sunday evenings without charge. (He does accept donations though, and you should consider offering one.) See him at Sedona Pines Resort and at the Hyatt.

Want the **spa experience** without paying resort prices? Call NAMTI (Northern Arizona Massage Training Institute) for a massage from the students and pay only $30. Their office is on Southwest Drive, off Hwy 89A in West Sedona.

Can't afford a round at the Sedona Golf Resort in the high season? The **executive course** at Canyon Mesa is much less expensive. Go small and cheap with **miniature golf** at Los Abrigados which costs but $5. For low-cost **history lessons**, visit the Sedona Heritage Museum off Jordan Road in Uptown.

There's one last way to try some activities in town at a discount: Sign on for a **timeshare tour**. (See the Accommodations chapter for local properties.) Note that they'll pre-qualify you by inquiring about your annual income. If it's not above $25,000 or so per year, you won't get the deal. And what is the deal? Usually it is a free jeep or biplane tour, a free meal, or a discounted stay at a local accommodation. Realize, however, that you're committed to hearing out the 90-minute pitch.

Q: How can we splurge in Sedona?

If money is truly no object, then read on for the best of the best in town. The first thing you need to do is to make sure you'll be here long enough to spend it. Once your flight is set, don't settle for just any rental car. Get yourself an escort from Red Rock Limousines.

The most important choice will be **where to stay**. Enchantment Resort in Boynton Canyon is your best bet if you'd like to relax in a gorgeous canyon. But don't settle for just any room in this lavish resort with at least five pools. Ask for Casita 31, the room with its own pool. Or stay for just a thousand dollars a night at Enchantment's new spa, Mii Amo, and the massage therapist will come to you. If you want something closer to town, try L'Auberge de Sedona. From Cabin 15 you can watch the ducks floating by on Oak Creek as you awake in the morning. However, if first class means "cozy," rely on Sedona's four-diamond bed & breakfasts. Be well treated at Adobe Village, part of the Graham property, located in the Village of Oak Creek.

To spare no expense, I'm afraid the jeep and trolley tours aren't pricey enough. Instead, fly above it all with an early morning **balloon ride** with Red Rock Balloon Adventures. Spectacular! Back on the ground, the chase crew will await your return with a champagne breakfast.

To explore more of Sedona once you're back on land, only an exclusive **private guide** will do. My own outings are the choice of discriminating visitors, who enjoy getting to know the little-known parts of Red Rock Country and have a lot of fun doing it. We'll enjoy a picnic in a most scenic spot. Want even better? Add fluteplayer Jesse Kalu to the mix: He'll be waiting, hidden in the forest to serenade us as we arrive at a sunny spot on the rocks.

For **dinner**, try the chateaubriand for two at Savannah's. Even better, order a **private meal** at The Cabin. If you can't put a price on privacy, they will.

It's been a wonderful weekend so far, but with so much more to spend, you may have to divide and conquer. Make arrangements for one of you to play a round at the Sedona Golf Resort, hiring the **teaching pro to play 18** with you. That means one of you hits the shops! There are those cute little **sculptures** in front of Exposures Gallery, and for a million or so you can have the white sculpture by Francis Jansen. Bring home one of nature's works of art too, with an exquisite **quartz crystal** from Crystal Magic. Pick up something **handmade** at Garland's Navajo Rugs to place under your treasures. For something more personal, visit Garland's sister store in Oak Creek Canyon for exceptional **silver jewelry** with turquoise and lapis inlays, or visit Geoffrey Roth, Ltd. at Tlaquepaque if you'd like something custom designed in **gold**.

When the golfing and shopping are over, take a break for a session at New Day Spa. Why settle for two hands when four are available with the Abhyanga and Shirodhara treatments? Two therapists will **massage** you with healing oils.

To finish, remember that no Sedona getaway is complete without a dose of esoterica. Try a **psychic reading** with Zeffi Kefala, who can predict what you'll have to do to pay for all this!

Approximate Prices for the Big Splurge

Sedona Golf Resort	$92.
Psychic reading by Zeffi Kefala	$150.
Serenade by fluteplayer Jesse Kalu	$250.
Red Rock Balloon Adventure	$300.
Deluxe Outing, Private Guide	$350.
New Day Spa treatments	$450.
Savannah's: cabin and dinner	$500.
Enchantment Resort: casita #31	$1,175.
Geoffrey Roth, Ltd: James Breski ring	$17,600.
Exposures gallery: sculpture	$1,200,000.

Q: What is the geology of Sedona?

Even if you've never been interested in the subject of geology, it's hard not to be curious about the story of Sedona's red rocks. Just how do these formations and these colors end up here? The truth is that much of the story remains a mystery, making it difficult to offer a precise, step-by-step account. What we do know are the broad outlines and that, my dear Watson, allows us to make it elementary.

WATER

Once upon a time, 350 million years ago, there was no Sedona, because the North American continent did not yet exist as we know it today. The ocean that was present laid down a foundation upon which later land would form. In subsequent eras, water would again and again fill the region and then retreat. The process of building up land—in seashores, lake beds, et cetera—and yet also eroding it away is the first part of the complex geological story.

EARTH

It was 225 million years ago that the land itself would take center stage. The terrain that existed—now closer in size to the North American continent that we know—was moving. Tectonic plates in the region collided and slid. To the north, their interaction is obvious, as they pushed up the Rocky Mountains. Around here something different occurred. The Pacific and North American plates scraped alongside each other, until the heavier of the two sank and lifted the lighter one above it. This created the Southwest's predominant land-mass, the Colorado Plateau, which extends into northern Arizona, southern Utah, western New Mexico and southwestern Colorado. In effect, on the escarpment of the plateau is Sedona, a place formed not from what was here, but from what was left behind.

The Arizona portion of the plateau's edge is known as the Mogollon Rim, named for a Spanish Colonial governor from the early 1700s, when the area was still part of New Spain. Mogollon (MUH-gee-yon) is a word that people have trouble pronouncing. We make it easier by simply calling it The Rim. It divides the sunny but chilly climate of northern Arizona from the warmer temperatures of the Verde Valley and the Valley of the Sun (Phoenix area).

FIRE

Even if you remembered enough grade school geology to deduce the presence of water and moving land, it is unlikely that you've stumbled upon the region's most interesting geological presence: volcanoes. There are more than 800, in fact, in the Colorado Plateau region. One of them was right here, and its eruption approximately eight million years ago led to massive flows of lava. For evidence, look to the top of Wilson Mountain, Sedona's highest peak, just north of Uptown. There you'll notice that above the red and blonde sandstone layers rests a chocolate-gray edge. It's basalt, the lava rock laid down several million years ago. Tougher and rougher than sandstone, it will last a lot longer than Sedona's colorful cliffs.

WIND

What of our final, missing element? The invisible wind has been at work all along. At times, the region was a vast area of massive sand dunes. As winds shifted, old dunes eroded while new ones were built up. This left a pattern of angular lines in the sand known as crossbeds. Eventually the dunes were cemented into sandstone by iron oxide with some calcium carbonate. On any sunny day you'll see the sparkle of the stones as a reminder of its sandy past.

Although Sedona isn't particularly windy (spring afternoons being the exception), the breezes that come pull specks of sandstone and smash them into other sandstone walls, slowly eroding them away. Geology happens.

So we come to Sedona today, a remarkable place in a transition zone between the snowy high country of the Colorado Plateau and the vast, dry Sonoran Desert. In an attempt to pull in elements of these two contrary regions we call it High Desert.

Q: What are the names of the rock formations?

It's a funny thing about the names of rocks in Sedona: many still have no name and others that do keep changing! The largest peak above West Sedona has been known by numerous names over the years, and you'll hear folks who have lived here a while calling it **Capitol Butte**. Today, however, **Thunder Mountain** has taken over.

The multi-spired peak known as **Cathedral Rock** was originally known as Courthouse Rock. The name was switched on an old USGS map. Except for a couple of Sedona's most long-lived residents, we've accepted the switch.

Coffee Pot, fortunately, is easy to see. It sits at the right edge (east) of the Thunder Mountain ridge. A steep cliff forms the right side of the pot, and a rock jutting further out forms its spout. (For the under-40 crowd, this is an old-fashioned percolater, not an automatic drip carafe.)

Of all the celebrities who have come and gone, **Snoopy** is our favorite. He lies on his back (on his doghouse, we presume) on the east side of town, visible from Uptown.

Bell Rock is named for its shape. If you don't think it looks like a bell, then use a little imagination! Find it on Hwy 179 just north of the Village of Oak Creek. Stately Courthouse Butte sits behind it to the east.

There are plenty more out there to find, from the fantastical (Mermaid) to the profane (Bill and Monica), cartoonish (Mr. Magoo, Homer Simpson), picturesque (The Mitten) and legendary (The Sphinx). Likewise, there are many more in search of a visitor with a good eye and a better imagination to give the name they've always wanted. Go to it

Q: What's so funny about getting to Sedona?

The most underrated pleasure of living in a tourist town is all the tourists I get to meet. It has been a joy to meet people from across the country and around the world. It's been just as much fun to see that a good sense of humor makes the journey even better. As an homage to tourists who have become visitors, visitors who have become guests, and guests who have become friends, here are some accent-friendly directions for getting to Sedona. Read them, if you can, with a provincial attitude (and accent) in mind.

ACCENT-FRIENDLY DIRECTIONS FROM DISTANT LOCATIONS

Los Angeles, California   7 to 14 hours. It depends.
Visualize this, dude. There is a land where mileage and the minutes to cross them are equivalent. Where you can actually go 20 miles in—get this—20 minutes! I fool you not! There are even stretches of highway where the speed limit is 75, and you can actually go that fast! I-40 East for 360 miles. Exit 113 B to 101 North for 20 miles. I-17 North for 85 miles. Hwy 179 for 15 miles. Oh, and bring me an In-N-Out Burger: They don't have any here.

San Francisco, California   12 hours, 15 minutes
No, don't do it. It's tempting, I know, but don't. Yes, it's a neighboring state, but don't do it. You'll regret it deeply by Bakersfield. Just fly. From Oakland, not SFO. It's sooo much easier. That's a call on my cell…gotta' go. Blackberry me when you get here.

Tulsa, Oklahoma   14 hours
Fourteen hours? Well that's just a Sunday drive, innit? Just start early. Of course, not till after service. You'd want God on your side for a long drive, rather than trying to short-change the Lord on His Day. And don't let me see you coming in the pickup. Take the Cadillac with the patriotic bumper-stickers. For directions, take a right at the First Baptist Church and a left at the Third Baptist Church, and

then follow the fence posts to I-40. Take it west until the car nearly runs out of gas, and the road-kill armadillos turn into to road-kill coyotes. Pick me up some ketchup at the Kwik Trips and holler when you get here. We'll keep the fried chicken and gravy ready for you all.

Baton Rouge, Louisiana   21 hours

I know, I know, why would you ever leave Louisiana? For one thing, the weather is more regular and for another the people are friendly. But you still can't be sure of whether they know how to have fun out there, so ya'll will want to stop at Fred's in Mamou. It's a little out of the way, but Papa and Mama will be there, and there's dancing on Saturday morning. Remember, we don't eat to live, we live to eat, and who knows if they've got good food out there, so grab some gumbo and jumbalaya. Take a right a Joe's pool hall and a left at the drive-through Daiquiri Shack onto 287. The directions from there are like Sister Catherine's math class: I-10 to I-20 to I-30 to I-40.

Chicago, Illinois   24 hours

Just think, this time tomorrow you could be in Sedona and THE CUBBIES PLAY SPRING TRAINING PRACTICALLY RIGHT DOWN THE BLOCK! Take 55 South to St. Louis, spit on a Cardinals fan, then follow 44 West to I-40 West, which you'll take FOREVER. Exit 195 sends you south on I-17 for a couple of miles, taking the Sedona/89A exit for the drive down Oak Creek Canyon. I know, I know, you want to know, "Which way is the lake?"

New York, New York   35 hours

Any New Yorker knows there's only question: "Which tunnel?" The Holland, of course. Through Jersey to the PA Turnpike, and bada-bing, bada-boom you're in Ohio. Now I-70 to I-55. Sure, there's traffic, but it beats the B.Q.E. after a Jets game. Okay I-40, where you can drive faster than Gene Hackman in the *French Connection* chase scene. Hey, 'dis country is humongous! When you're ready to puke if you don't see signs of civilization, look for the mountain with white stuff on top. ("Snow? I thought this was freakin' Arizona?") Fuhgeddabbouddit. By the way, could you bring me a bagel and *The Daily News*?

Guided Tours with Mr. Sedona

In picking Sedona, "America's Most Beautiful Destination," you've made a choice that suggests you expect the best that life offers. So, how will you spend your precious time? Standing in line, shoved into a crowd, or lost on the streets? If so, then you'll be living your vacation by someone else's rules.

Instead, choose the private experience that connects you with the thrilling beauty and peaceful serenity of Sedona. Escape the crowds and pavement for the silence and panoramas of the Red Rocks. Your enjoyment is absolutely guaranteed. For informative tours, exciting hikes and magical vortex adventures for couples, families, individuals and small groups, choose Mr. Sedona. For more information check the website at: www.MrSedona.com.

Media sources mentioning or recommending Mr. Sedona's outings include: The USA Network, The Weather Channel, The Family Travel Forum, CBS-5 Phoenix, FOX TV Phoenix, *The San Francisco Chronicle, Scottsdale Magazine* and *Every Day with Rachael Ray. Frommer's Budget Travel* said, "Dennis Andres is a gifted guide and an endless resource."

Call: 928-204-2201
Advance reservations are essential.

Get Updated Information on Our Website

Some information changes so fast that it can't be printed in a book. So where can you find it?

If you've purchased this book, you'll be able to access the latest critical reviews of accommodations and restaurants, our picks for massage therapist and alternative health care providers and the scoop on conditions outdoors.

Sedona: The Essential Guidebook isn't just the only guide book to Sedona. It's also the only one that guarantees that you'll stay in-the-know on what's new in Red Rock Country!

Even better, you'll have a chance to contribute your feedback so that others can benefit from your experience. Log on to tell others about your stay in the area.

Visit our website today:

www.MrSedona.com

In memoriam, Phillip Fife.

About the Author

Dennis Andres is Mr. Sedona. A former diplomat, development volunteer and management consultant, he has lived or worked on five continents and speaks six languages. As an outdoor guide, he has led clients from Machu Picchu to Mt. Everest, Tuscany to Tibet, but finds the most pleasure in a hike around Sedona. A dedicated meditator for two decades, he is an expert on Sedona's vortex energy, a certified yoga instructor and personal coach. Meanwhile, his experience in real estate and investing help him to serve others who choose to make the Red Rocks their home too. A proponent of nature and the arts, he has contributed his time, money and talent to a number of local charitable organizations. Writer and humorist, Dennis is the author of the best-selling book *What is a Vortex?* and the award-winning *Sedona's Top 10 Hikes*.

Other Sedona books by Dennis Andres

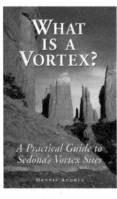

Gain insights into Sedona's positive energy!

This practical guide provides directions to Sedona's vortex sites and gives answers to often asked questions.

What Is A Vortex?
$8.95

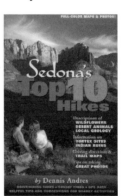

Sedona's most in-depth trail companion!

This award-winning hike book, filled with full-color maps and photos, is both beautiful and descriptive.

Sedona's Top 10 Hikes
$11.95

To order books contact: **Dreams In Action Distribution**
e-mail: orders@DreamsInAction.us   **web site:** www.DreamsInAction.us
phone: (928) 204-1560   **write:** P.O. Box 1894, Sedona AZ 86339